PIECES OF THE PUZZLE

PIECES
OF THE
PUZZLE

The Power of Divine Providence

Rivkah Leah Jacobs

TARGUM/FELDHEIM

First published 2003
Copyright © 2003 by Rivkah Leah Jacobs
ISBN 1-56871-246-4

Published by:
TARGUM PRESS, INC.
22700 W. Eleven Mile Rd.
Southfield, MI 48034
E-mail: targum@netvision.net.il
Fax: 888-298-9992
www.targum.com

Distributed by:
FELDHEIM PUBLISHERS
202 Airport Executive Park
Nanuet, NY 10954

Printed in Israel

Rabbi Zev Leff

Rabbi of Moshav Matityahu
Rosh Hayeshiva Yeshiva Gedola Matisahu
D. N. Modi'in 71917 Tel. (08) 976-1138 Fax. (08) 976-5326

I have read the manuscript of *Pieces of the Puzzle* by Rivkah Leah Jacobs, לאי״ט. Rabbi and Mrs. Jacobs are longtime, very close friends of mine (as is mentioned in the book). They are people who live an exemplary Torah life and constantly seek ways to benefit the community. Mrs. Jacobs presents her memories of her father, ז״ל, and the ordeal of her son's accident in a manner that evokes belief and faith in the Creator, love and fear of Him, and a pride in Torah and *Yiddishkeit* engendered by the mitzvah of revering one's parents and the love of a parent for a child.

I recommend this book as an enjoyable source of inspiration and strength.

With Torah blessings,

Zev Leff

A tribute
to my father,
Shlomo Meir ben Chaim Yehuda

Contents

Book Three My Father's Inner Strength

Preface

Honoring one's parents, *kibbud av va'eim*, is a positive commandment from the holy Torah. It should not be taken lightly, since it is one of the few mitzvos whose reward is specifically stated in the Torah: "that your days may be lengthened." The following true stories are vivid examples of this mitzvah and its reward. The main characters I can proudly claim to be my family members.

From all of the 613 mitzvos that have been bestowed upon the Jewish people, ten were stated in the Ten Commandments. Engraved into the stone tablets that Moshe Rabbeinu brought with him as he descended from Har Sinai were the words that exemplify our relationship with our Creator. This was only the beginning, as the complete Torah is our guidebook for life. This gift, presented to us as a nation, enables us to serve our Creator and fulfill our mission in this world.

Of the Ten Commandments, five of them are positive and five negative. The Creator of the Universe has dictated that we shall not murder or steal. Observing the negative ordinances puts a hold on our *yetzer hara*, like pulling the reins on a horse, requiring us to hold back any form of immoral behavior. On a positive note, we are instructed to keep the Sabbath, as well as to honor our mother and father. By doing so, we also honor the Master of the Universe. Observing the positive commandments assures us a peaceful and respectable way of life.

Unfortunately, until the third and final Beis HaMikdash will be built, we are unable to fulfill all of the 613 commandments and must suffice with those that are within our jurisdiction at the current time. The mitzvah of honoring our mother and father is one that most of us can fulfill. Telephone calls, letters, e-mails, and visits all fit into the category of this injunction. Standing up for a parent when he walks into the room, showing respect in any manner, refraining from correcting him, and not sitting in his or her chair, all constitute this positive commandment.

If we work on ourselves, we can make strides in the fulfillment of this mitzvah. It can be difficult at times, but with practice and extra effort, we can attain near perfection. One never knows how many days he is given in this world; therefore, any extension of life is a bonus. I extend a *berachah* that all of *klal Yisrael* should have the *zechus* to fulfill this mitzvah and receive the blessing of extended days.

I'd like to thank my dear husband, Yeshaya, for his patience, and my wonderful children for their interest in my work and for allowing me to read, reread, and even translate into Hebrew the parts they didn't understand in the book. I'd also like to express my appreciation to the Targum staff and all the people involved in bringing this book to fruition, particularly Rabbi Dombey, Miriam Zakon, D. Liff, who produced a beautiful cover, and Chaya Baila Gavant. Many hours have been spent on proofreading, technical adjustments, and other behind-the-scenes aspects of this book.

May we all be granted the "gift" of Mashiach, speedily in our times.

27 Shevat, 5763
(January 30, 2003)

Introduction

Every person's life experiences are intertwined with the magnificent phenomenon of Divine providence. If one looks for God's intervention, he will undoubtedly find it. To appreciate the puzzle that the Creator has set before us, it's just a matter of seeing how all the pieces fit into place.

Instead of taking for granted the fact that we can walk, breathe, eat, and so forth, we can open up our eyes and ears and recognize how special these natural capabilities are. It shouldn't have to take, *chas vechalilah*, a tragedy for us to place value on all the things we are given, with God's grace.

The story I recall in Book One, "The Soup Lady," presents an example of how our Creator intercedes on our behalf, focusing on the power of charity to save one's life. I would like to demonstrate how our lifestyles will have a direct effect on the future generations of *klal Yisrael*. As parents, it is up to every one of us to involve ourselves in creating a lasting impression on our children. Fathers and mothers have the opportunity to set precedents for the future generation by defining guidelines and serving as examples for their offspring.

In Book Two, "My Son's Accident," I share another personal experience which aims to magnify the reader's understanding of Divine intervention. My son's life was thankfully spared through Hashem's great kindness, and it is my hope that the story will serve as an inspiration for many.

Finally, in Book Three, "My Father's Inner Strength," I recall an experience so obviously guided from Heaven that it would be a shame not to share it. When I was sitting shivah, people came to offer condolences, both in the United States and in Israel. They came to strengthen me, but left with the feeling that I gave them the real *chizuk* with my true life experience. I told a few of the women that I was seriously thinking about writing a book and was told, "You must write about it! It's unbelievable!"

The way that we behold life is most likely the way our children will as well. By pointing out the daily miracles to our children, we have the opportunity to foster their appreciation of perpetual Divine intervention. In *Shemoneh Esrei*, we say, "*Unesaper...al nisecha shebechol yom imanu* — And we will tell about the miracles You perform for us every day." Sometimes people become oblivious to what is going on around them. If one takes the time to frequently search for the Almighty's touch upon everything in this vast universe, one will come to revere His Divine presence.

Book One

THE SOUP LADY

CHAPTER 1

Three Percent

Fall, 1983

"What do you mean, doctor?" I asked, aghast.

"I mean that your blood results are higher than normal, and it is necessary to take a certain drug in order to lower them before you can successfully bear another child." The professor enunciated his words as a matter of fact.

I gathered my inner strength. "But Professor Ben David, I am already expecting my next child. I received the good news just yesterday."

The doctor rose up to his full height, and then he shook his head.

I knew about his expertise on this particular problem. He had developed the ideas and formulated the testing. My next inquiry was a tough one. "What are my chances, according to the statistics, of carrying through this pregnancy?"

Running his fingers through his thick brown hair, he contemplated and let out a sigh, studying me almost pityingly. "About three percent."

With a sinking feeling, I drew in a deep breath and whispered, "Thank you for your help." My husband's eyes met mine and we quietly left the office. Was this a time to sulk? Would I allow the doctor's words to get the better part of me? I firmly answered myself, *No!*

My mind was put into full gear. I knew that it had not been a coincidence that twice, once before Yom Kippur and the other time before Pesach, the baby I had been carrying had not reached its destination here on this earth. Although both pregnancies had been in the early stages, their natural termination had filled me with devastation.

I had cried to my dear faithful friend, Esther. She had strengthened me through her kind, gentle, and encouraging words. "Don't worry! Everything will be all right. You're still young, and you have plenty of time to have many more children. Be thankful for the ones you do have, and, *b'ezras Hashem*, you'll be blessed with many more."

I decided that this time I must do something special. It is written that *tzedakah* saves one from death. Distributing money, however, would mean that the beneficiary would have to buy what he needed himself. That wouldn't do. I had to make some contribution that would really make a difference. If I would prepare food, supplying the recipient with immediate gratification, it would be considered a higher form of *tzedakah*. I felt that I had to do everything in my power to try to annul any decree that might have been declared against my unborn baby. Prayers and supplications would also be needed. I knew that I could count on the cooperation of my brother and his wife, as well as my sister-in-law and her husband, to daven for me. Both sets of parents would not be notified for the time being. Causing them unnecessary worry could aggravate the situation.

Before approaching our house, my wonderful husband, Yeshaya, broke the silence. "What are you thinking about? Do you want to share it with me?"

"You know, Shaya, I used to make meals to help new mothers. It's a bit too time-consuming now, as I have teaching responsibilities in addition to the children to care of, but I'd like to start making soups. It's a whole meal in one; the families would only have to add bread."

"It's a fine idea and a tremendous *chesed*," he replied, easing the car into its parking place.

I needed to buy beans, barley, and vegetables of all shapes, sorts, and colors as soon as possible to start my "soup-making project." I would check the announcements in the local news bulletin, distributed weekly, for anyone who had just given birth. My spouse and children would be on call for regular deliveries.

My project succeeded in teaching my own children the value of the *middah* of *chesed*. Youngsters learn from acts that their parents perform. Speech is not enough to make an impression on young minds; actually demonstrating *chesed* is. Practicing what you preach is the best way to impart a message. Putting my efforts into this mitzvah and doing it with joy could prove to be the best way to annul the decree against my unborn child.

I can happily say that many years later I was able to witness the fruits of my labor. When I phoned my oldest married daughter one morning, she had to cut our conversation a bit short. When I inquired about her hurry, she answered, "Mommy, I'm busy making soup for my neighbor, who just had a baby!"

This is all part of Hashem's perpetual puzzle. Even when we think that the puzzle pieces have all been placed, it seems to continue to grow endlessly, from one generation to the next.

Sometimes what appears to be a hindrance to us, with our

limited knowledge, is really our greatest asset. It isn't always crystal clear what Hashem has planned for us or how He will manifest His will into our daily lives, but looking for His Divine Intervention can clarify many things.

I can still recall the day in the English superintendent's office....

CHAPTER 2

Completion Course

August, 1983

I walked confidently into the English supervisor's office with my acceptance letters from the Amalya Girls' High School and the Jinogly Religious High School in hand. The superintendent perused my records and then looked me squarely in the face. "I'm sorry, Mrs. Jacobs, but you may not have the job."

It took a few seconds to fully absorb the ramification of his declaration. "I — I don't understand. The principals of both of these schools accepted me as a teacher for this coming school year. I have all the credentials, including a Bachelor's degree from Ohio State University, American and Israeli teaching certificates, and years of teaching experience. I am a highly qualified teacher!"

"Yes, that is correct; however, you did not take the completion course that is necessary to enable you to fill either of these positions."

"Sir, I was specifically informed that it could be postponed until next summer, because I was teaching a course this summer."

He raised his voice with authority. "Whoever gave you that

piece of information was seriously mistaken, as I am the only one who can give such a deferment, and I am not allowing it. That is all for now." Twitching his nose and pointing a bony finger to the door, he called out, "Next!"

Totally confounded, I walked away with a heavy heart. I'd had my heart set on teaching English in these two schools. I sensed that I could be successful with these students; now it would be put on a back burner. I was left with a mere six-hour-a-week job, teaching art history in a prestigious girls' high school. To me it seemed that I'd just been demoted.

Would my extra hours be filled with boredom? Would I have been able to fulfill my duties and role as a professional teacher?

As the time passed, the answers to my questions began to surface.

February, 1984

I waddled like a duck. Some of the small schoolchildren mocked me, unaware that I could hear them. "Look at her. She walks just like a duck. Ha, ha," they jeered.

The physical pain from my sciatic nerve was annoying, causing me to walk in such an off-balance fashion. I thought of how thankful I was, to travel on the bus only once a week to my six-hour teaching job. Then it dawned on me.

The English supervisor, as mean and nasty as he appeared to be at the time, was only doing his job. He was acting as a messenger of the Ribbono shel Olam, in preventing me from taking on a responsibility that would have been impossible for me to carry through from my sixth month of pregnancy onward. It would have been very distressful to notify both schools that I had to leave my teaching position because of lack of physical strength caused by my aggravated sciatic nerve. A piece of the puzzle had been put into place.

We don't always get such clear-cut pictures, but whether we do or not, we have to realize that Hashem constantly intervenes on our behalf, and show our appreciation.

One frosty winter morning, an extra large pot of bean and barley soup stood proudly on the rear black grate of my stove. It sent a savory aroma all over the house. The slamming of the front door followed the arrival of happy-go-lucky Nechemyah, who was quite hungry.

"Ima, the soup smells great!" He pulled up his chair and was served promptly.

Like most families in Israel, we had no microwave oven. A few years earlier, when Nechemyah's hunger drew him home, he would demand his food immediately. I would tell him that it had to be warmed up, but he'd demand to eat it cold. "I'm hungry now." I got used to his growth spurts and tried to have some edibles ready when he needed it. Now I could serve him immediately.

Nechemyah washed his hands and recited the *berachah HaMotzi* before taking some of the bread that was on the table. "How come the other pot is so big today?" he inquired curiously between swallows.

"Honey, you know the Ben Dahan family, don't you?"

"Sure."

"Both the mother and the father are ill, and I thought it would be a great mitzvah to send a larger than usual pot of soup to them. It will provide them with a bit extra to use for a few days."

My son nodded his head. He was happy to share in this mitzvah by helping his father. After he finished eating, Yeshaya drove over to the Ben Dahans with Nechemyah, who balanced the soup pot on a large towel on his lap and delivered it safely to its destination.

Although I proudly watched my children developing in their service of Hashem, at the same time I worried over my health and the progress of my pregnancy. Would the Ribbono shel Olam grant me another healthy baby?

CHAPTER 3

Sewing the Final Touches

April, 1984

My pregnancy was advancing. My prayers continued, and I couldn't conceal my happiness, having made it into the eighth month without complications.

My closest friend, Esther, continued to encourage me through thick and thin. She used various tactics to help me forget the past and look forward to a positive future.

Esther decided to go on a sewing binge just before Pesach (as if the cleaning wasn't enough). She felt it was a healthy, constructive way to take a break, yet utilize our energies positively. I would frequently bring my iron to her house so that she'd sew and I'd complete my ironing while we shared various experiences.

This time she taught me how to cut and prepare patterns by using old newspapers. I also had some ready-made patterns that I'd brought with me when we made aliyah. She proceeded to design, cut, and sew new outfits for all of her girls, as well as a dress for herself.

Rebbetzin Minhahar, her mother, had taught her to sew at a young age. Sewing was an essential part of the household in which she had grown up, in Yerushalayim. She had lived in the Old City before Esther was born without a refrigerator, washing machine, or other basics. My American-born, Canadian-bred mother had possessed these "luxuries" even as a child.

Rebbetzin Minhahar received her first small icebox, to keep the milk from spoiling, as a gift from her husband when they had their sixth child. Running water was not available either, so the local Arab had to bring them a large barrel of water daily. It was used for drinking, bathing, cooking, scrubbing dishes, and finally for washing the floor. Water was rationed, not wasted.

We experienced a three-week water shortage in Beit El. Esther gave me a present — the book her sister, Puah Steiner, had written, *Mitoch HaHafechah* (later translated into English under the title *Forever, My Jerusalem*). It was the first Hebrew book I'd ever read (other than *sifrei kodesh*). Its influence got me through the water shortage. True, we had no water available during the daylight hours, but faucets brought forth an abundant amount of it during the evening and night. I could use my washing machine, give the children baths, and fill up pots, pitchers, and basins of water in preparation for the next day without even having to step foot out of the house. I learned to appreciate running water and stop taking it for granted.

Esther was born in Old Katamon, where the family sewing tradition had been passed on to her. Bought clothing was almost unheard of, sold at exorbitant prices. Sewing the children's apparel was just as common as cooking. By the time their family moved to Bayit Vegan, she'd already become quite experienced in sewing.

Our sewing sessions proved quite valuable, and Esther found solutions whenever I came up against a seemingly unsolvable snag. Sewing was not only challenging, but it also kept me busy.

At the time, Esther had only one son, and she opted to buy his white shirt and dress pants for Pesach. I was quite determined to utilize all of my newly acquired sewing skills and use the material I'd brought from America in my lift. I stitched skirts and vests for my daughters and a maternity jumper for myself. There was no time to travel to the city to purchase white material, so I took a new white sheet and cut shirt patterns. I invested many days in stitching two white shirts with starched collars and teal blue pants for my sons.

Exasperated, my husband asked, "Why can't we just buy them the shirts?" He was beginning to feel sorry for me, as I was going to bed much later than usual.

"The joy they'll feel at having their mother sew the clothing for them will be worth it," I answered calmly. After embroidering each boy's initial in yellow thread on the inner side of his garments, I handed my sons the pants and shirts, which had taken some fifty hours to complete.

"Wow! Ima, you really made these for us? This is better than any shirt you could ever have bought for us. Thanks!" Nechemyah said, happily planting a kiss on my cheek.

"Ima, you're terrific. Thanks!" Avdiel echoed, also pecking my cheek. They both hurried from the room to try on their new clothing.

I was pleased; it had been a real success.

When Pesach arrived, the table was set with the sparkling cutlery and silver Kiddush cups. Eliyahu HaNavi's tall, wide, silver goblet, filled to the brim with red wine, towered above the rest next to the round seder plate. Everyone came to the seder wearing brand new *yom tov* finery; I sat regally like a queen surrounded by my little princes and princesses, while my king sat on his throne opposite me.

The eighth month of pregnancy made it more difficult than

usual to eat all the required seder foods. Our neighbor sent us some Sefardi pita-type matzah, which tasted like a rubber tire. My other choice was munching on "cardboard" — the Ashkenazi-type matzah. Regardless, I was glad to fulfill the mitzvah of eating matzah on Pesach, though it meant pushing my rounded abdomen to its limits, and drink the obligatory four cups of wine (in my case, grape juice).

❋   ❋   ❋

My husband was called to the army reserves from the first day of Chol HaMoed Pesach. I knew that it wouldn't be easy to be without him for the end of the *chag*, but invitations were plentiful; my children and I wouldn't be alone.

Fortunately, our kind *ben bayis*, Yitzchak, came over straightaway after the end of the *chag* to help pack the Pesach dishes. A tall, slim fellow with thick wire-rimmed glasses, he rolled up his sleeves and got busy. (Yitzchak frequented our house as a Shabbos guest along with other English-speaking yeshivah students that my husband taught. It was always our pleasure to extend an invitation for Shabbos meals.)

My children were as helpful as possible, and around midnight, we had our kitchen back in order. Although the bakeries in Yerushalayim would have hot scrumptious bread on their shelves by about 1:00 A.M., most people would wait until daybreak to avoid the late night (or early morning) crowds.

What I didn't know about (until his return a few weeks later) was my husband's holiday in Lebanon....

CHAPTER 4

Pesach in Lebanon

My husband and David Koenigsberg were two fairly new *olim* from the United States who had chosen to take a communications course about a year prior to the dismantling of the systems in Lebanon. They were sent to the eastern sector that Pesach to help with the disassembling. (They had also been on duty earlier to erect the transmission system.)

There were many types of people amongst the group of soldiers, who came from varied backgrounds and countries of origin. Yeshaya and David, with their beards and black yarmulkes, were the most religious of the group.

Several days after they arrived, the captain approached David and Yeshaya. "I'm sorry to have to let you guys know this," he began sadly, "but there doesn't seem to be any chance of getting a *sefer Torah* to the group for the last day of Pesach."

David and Yeshaya looked at one another, raised their eyebrows, shrugged their shoulders, and thought, *Things could be worse.* Jewish soldiers have had to fight in armies all over the world under various stressful spiritual circumstances, and as it was Pesach they felt fortunate to be in the Israeli army. They were not exposed to any type of *chametz.* Only *Pesachdik* products, including an abundance of matzahs, were distributed at the bases around Israel.

Yeshaya spoke up. "Captain, we understand. We'll make do with our siddurim and lead a davening even without a *sefer Torah*."

Suddenly, a lanky Israeli named Gabi who supported a small crocheted yarmulke rose up and shouted, "What! You must bring us a Torah scroll!" He jumped up and down wildly, throwing his arms in the air. "We are in a Jewish army! Do you think we will settle for any meager excuse? You are our captain, and we follow your orders on the battlefield. Now you make sure that we get a Torah scroll to read from on Pesach!"

David and Yeshaya stood on the sidelines, gawking in amazement.

Two hours before sunset, to the astonishment of all the soldiers, a *sefer Torah* was flown in by helicopter. When the minyan was formed in the morning, Gabi had a beaming smile on his face.

David and Yeshaya had been ready to accept the circumstances, but Gabi had not. The lesson was clear enough. Where there is a will, there is a way; and don't look at the exterior of the jug, but what's inside it. The presence of the precious *sefer Torah* was accredited to Gabi.

Most of the soldiers in their particular group were callous, beardless, and hatless. Their language was coarse; they led a different lifestyle. Most were used to the cold weather and the rough conditions of life in a tent. To my husband's pleasant surprise, on Shabbos morning, the soldiers, who gobbled down their food voraciously without reciting a *berachah* during the week, waited patiently to hear Kiddush before commencing their meal. Shabbos Kodesh ignited their spark of *Yiddishkeit*.

On occasion (generally on weekdays) one of the soldiers would come to my husband's tent to ask him to gather a minyan for *benching gomel*. Whenever they narrowly missed a mine explosion or experienced any such incident, they expressed their gratitude to the Almighty by reciting *Birkas HaGomel* with a quorum.

Once, when Yeshaya was awaiting the bus headed for Israel's farthest northern point, near the Lebanese border, a soldier shyly asked him, "Could I don your tefillin?"

Yeshaya was in a quandary. If he were to give the tefillin, he'd miss his bus, but, on the other hand, if he didn't offer them, he would miss his chance to perform a mitzvah. When would this soldier lay tefillin? He opted for the former, handing the soldier his siddur as well.

When the soldier completed his prayers, my husband carefully wound up his phylacteries and sat down on a nearby stoop to wait for a ride. He didn't have long to ponder on his decision. An army vehicle pulled up and the driver bellowed, "Need a ride?"

"Yes, I do. Any chance that you're heading in the direction of the northern departure point to Lebanon?"

"We sure are," answered the drive, smiling.

Loading his cumbersome equipment into the jeep, Yeshaya hopped in. After about an hour of riding, he saw his crew, carrying all of their heavy equipment, trudging up the long road, where they would wait for final transportation at the border crossing. The bus had transported the group as far as possible, leaving them to walk the last few kilometers with all of their accouterments. The vehicle that was carrying my husband sped along, right past the entire group of soldiers, directly to the meeting place to await the transport. Thus my husband was the first, rather than the last, to arrive at his destination. Hashem offered him an appropriate and deserving reward.

Yeshaya was given furlough on Israeli Independence Day and arrived home at dusk. The children smothered him with hugs, kisses, and warm greetings. I noticed that his hair had begun to turn gray, and I could well imagine what he had gone through.

After the little ones had been tucked into bed, Yeshaya told me how arduous those few weeks had been. The folks in the States had not been informed of Yeshaya's whereabouts, so they wouldn't have to worry. I told them that he was stationed near the northern border (which was true — I just didn't elaborate on which side of the border).

"Rivkah, there were times when I went to sleep at night not knowing if I'd wake up the next morning. I wasn't convinced that I'd ever see you or the children again. Every morning I concentrated on *Modeh Ani*, appreciating every second of my precious life that much more."

"We missed you, davened for you, and thought about you constantly. *Baruch Hashem*, you're back safe and sound."

CHAPTER 5

The Dream

I t was the end of my eighth month when I had the dream. I couldn't remember any of it except for one single detail. The name *Elishama* had been screamed numerous times. "Elishama, Elishama, Elishama." I heard it over and over again. It had reached a crescendo when I woke up in a cold sweat, shaking like a leaf. My mouth was dry; my palms were beaded with moisture. Although it was still the middle of the night, I had difficulty falling asleep again.

I had safely completed seven months of pregnancy, was enduring the eighth, and would soon be entering the ninth. I was constantly thankful to my Creator for His kindness and His vigil.

Elishama sounded like a very beautiful name. I knew that it was the name of one of the *nesi'im* in the book of *Bemidbar*. I thought about it for awhile, with the dream so fresh in my mind, until I finally drifted back to sleep.

I related the dream to Yeshaya in the morning. He listened with raised eyebrows, but didn't put too much emphasis on it.

I continued with my soup contributions to every family in the neighborhood that had a *mazal tov*. Many new babies, *baruch Hashem*, were born weekly in Beit El Bet, the settlement where we lived. The number of residents was growing by leaps and bounds.

When we first moved to the *yishuv*, we were the forty-third family, and only forty-two telephone lines had been laid.

When the phone company personnel knocked on the door of our caravan and asked, "Did you order this phone?" I was tempted to say yes, but I would be taking the last phone line away from a family that had arrived before us. My conscience would never let me get away with such an answer.

"No," I admitted, "it was not our order." I watched him walk away with the coveted phone, knowing that we would be left without a phone for an indefinite period of time. (Distribution of phone lines had been discontinued until further notice.)

Soon after, we moved to the house that we built. When we first settled in our newly constructed home, it was situated at a distance from the other families, on an unoccupied, deserted street. None of the neighbors had moved into their new residences yet. We had no choice but to move because my parents were due to arrive on Sunday, and the small trailer we had lived in until then could not accommodate all of us.

According to the ruling of Rav Zalman Melamed, *rosh yeshivah* of Beit El, we had to moved into the house on Friday, *erev Shabbos*, as the Nine Days were approaching and this is an inauspicious time for the Jewish people. We had only a single day to move, a difficult feat which we accomplished under duress. Fortunately, we were invited to friends and former neighbors for all the Shabbos meals; we were not yet connected to electricity, nor to running water. Sleeping in the house was necessary in order to show possession of our newly acquired home.

Now the population had reached approximately 125 families.

Sometimes I would personally take the pot of soup to the woman who had just given birth. This would give me the chance to visit the mother and wish her *mazal tov* and also behold the newborn, letting the mother *kvell* with *nachas* over her new addition.

Every time I take a peek into the carriage of an infant, I stop to think about the miracles of creation. A *neshamah* has been brought down to the earth in order to fulfill its mission. It will have to go through many trials and tribulations and hopefully fulfill the purpose for which it was created.

A healthy baby is born with ten fingers and toes, the ability to breathe, an enormous sucking power, the energy to kick his small legs, and eyes that are beginning to absorb his surroundings. His body is filled with just the right amount of fluids and blood. His bones are all in place, veins and vital organs are functioning, the brain is working, and the potential to grow into an adult is there from the instant he enters this world.

Every Jewish baby is so sweet and pure. A new, fresh life soft skin, which can grow into a robust, brilliant, God-fearing Jew — a boy who will pore over the sacred books, or a girl who will grow to be a *bas Yisrael* taking pride in being a mother and raising her family.

"Your baby is beautiful. May you raise him to the Torah, the *chuppah*, and good deeds. I wish you *mazal tov* and much *nachas*," I would say. I knew that the baby's mother would feel an extra gladness in her heart when I left, and I looked forward to the blessings from the One Above, who had it within His power to grant a new life to me in the near future. When we pray for others first, Hashem answers our own prayers.

One afternoon, after returning from a soup delivery, my

husband said, "When I knocked on Rutie's door, she smiled and said, 'Your wife doesn't forget anyone, does she?' She seemed very touched that you had remembered her."

"How could I not?" My friend Rutie, who had just given birth, was pleasant and vivacious, and her husband was a known *talmid chacham* always either writing *sifrei kodesh* or immersed in learning Torah. It was my honor to make soup for my friend and her family. (At a later date, when I'd have my next baby, Rutie would make me the best couscous we ever ate. She wanted to repay my kindness with one of her own.)

I was approaching the final stretch. It was the first week of May, the Hebrew month of Sivan, and the flowers were in full bloom.

CHAPTER 6

Final Stretch

The gardener, Nir, made sure to keep the bushes well trimmed and the flowerbeds weeded. Red and pink roses, yellow chrysanthemums, purple violets, white irises, and a variety of other flowers decorated the yeshivah grounds. Sweat poured from his brow as the sun beat down heavily. Looking at him, dressed in a *kova temble* (an Israeli sun hat), T-shirt, and short pants, you might think him to be a simple, stocky individual, but I knew differently. Rising before dawn to attend an early morning *shiur* with the *rosh yeshivah*, he then proceeded to the *vasikin minyan* and then had some breakfast before beginning his gardening job. I counted my blessings living in Eretz Yisrael and highly valued our *frum* gardener.

On Friday morning, 11 Sivan (May 31), the birth pangs began. I sent the children to school with their lunches and left to the hospital with Yeshaya. Wisely, I had already registered in Misgav Ladach Hospital; all necessary forms would be ready upon arrival. Although it was an older hospital, it was known for its American-style patient treatment. The hospital staff encouraged the childbirth methods the women preferred. I personally endorsed natural childbirth.

The knowledgeable and motherly midwife, Rachel, made me feel confident in her hands. Doctors were always available if any complication should arise, but the well-trained midwives were exceedingly competent.

Less than two hours after our arrival, we heard the newborn's cries.

"It's a boy!"

A healthy baby boy entered the world. To me, he was the most beautiful baby on earth. His tiny body was moving, including all of his tiny fingers and toes. Thin strands of blonde hair covered his small delicate head. His presence rendered me awestricken.

As soon as I washed my hands, I recited, *"Baruch atah Hashem Elokeinu melech ha'olam hatov v'hameitiv."*

When Yeshaya pronounced, *"Amein,"* I cried from happiness. A miracle had been performed for us. No words could describe our joy.

My husband had to hurry to buy all the necessities for the evening's *shalom zachor* and take care of the children. Fortunately, I cooked for Shabbos on Thursday.

Popcorn, chickpeas, nuts, pumpkin seeds, and assorted cakes were carefully laid out on the table after the *seudah.* Men's voices filled our living room with song, and my husband expressed his thankfulness and gratitude to the Almighty for granting us another son.

Our new son had been born in the parashah of *Naso* where the name Elishama ben Ehud is mentioned. Incredible! I had dreamt about Elishama. The name is mentioned in only two parashiyos; the one in which he was born, and the one which his bris would follow. A large piece of the puzzle had just been neatly put into place.

❋   ❋   ❋

On Sunday, we spoke about the name. "There's no question in my mind that we must give him the name Elishama," I told Yeshaya. "It means, 'my God heard.' My prayers have been answered. Beyond the shadow of a doubt, his *neshamah* had to be brought into the world and given this name. The dream I had is still reverberating in my head."

"Of course, we'll call him Elishama, but as all of our other children have two names, I'd like him to have a second name as well." Yeshaya's tone was kind. "I just recently returned from *Milchemet Shlom HaGalil*, and I'd like to use the name Shalom, as Hashem allowed me to come home safely. It was also, according to my mother, one of my great-grandfather's names."

The following Friday morning our son was named at his bris. Rav Zalman Melamed was his *sandek*. Rabbi Amiel Sternberg (my friend Esther's husband) recited the *berachah* with our new son's name. "And his name shall be called in the nation of Israel — Elishama Shalom."

EPILOGUE

Two years later my daughter, Miryam Dina, was born. Six weeks after her birth, on *erev Rosh HaShanah*, I took her to the pediatrician for her routine vaccination.

I'd been sick, supposedly with the flu, for a week. After examining the baby, the doctor, known for his expertise in the medical field, glanced at my face and proceeded to pull down my lower eyelids. He announced, "You have hepatitis!"

I was told to get into bed and rest, which was nearly devastating, as all the *yom tov* cooking still had to be done. As soon as I arrived home, calls began coming in, letting me know that our holiday preparations were well under way. By the evening our kitchen was full of kugels, cakes, chicken, salads, and more, all sent by our neighbors.

I realized that not only had charity saved my unborn child from death, but the mitzvos had also been recorded for a later time. It was my turn to receive other people's *chesed*. Hashem is very exacting in repaying our good deeds in many ways. May the Almighty continue to grant *am Yisrael* the ability to constantly participate in acts of kindness.

Book Two

MY SON'S ACCIDENT

CHAPTER 1

Request for *Tehillim*

I t was 6:45 P.M. on Sunday, just after the conclusion of Chanukah, 1995, when the phone rang in the Kurz home.

"Hello, Mom. It's Chaim."

"Chaim, I'm so glad you called," Dina, his mother, said cheerfully. She positioned the receiver between her ear and shoulder so that her hands would be free to prepare sandwiches for her brood of boys, due to arrive any moment.

Seriously, Chaim said, "Mom, I know you've already finished saying *Tehillim* today, but can you take out your *Sefer Tehillim* again and recite a few chapters for Avdiel Yitzchak ben Rivkah Leah?"

Almost dropping the receiver as she recognized the name, Dina exclaimed with alarm, "What happened?"

"He's — he's been in a terrible car accident. The entire yeshivah is gathering together to say *Tehillim* for him. The ambulance driver came from Mitzpeh Yericho; we were notified immediately. Mom, one more thing, whatever you do, please don't call the Jacobses, as they don't know yet."

CHAPTER 2

Desert Oasis

Sunday morning, the last day of Chanukah

It was 7:30 A.M. Backpack in position, gear in order, Avdiel was leaving the house to teach the last day of his course in mountain rappelling. "Ima," he said, "I'm planning on being home fairly early, *b'ezras Hashem*, since today is the last day of Chanukah, and I'd like to give the kiddies a little attention."

Avdiel paused, deep in thought, then added, "You know, it's interesting, but Shai, the youngest boy in my group, told me that his mother was frightened about this mountain rappelling course. Shai told her that more people die in car accidents than by mountain rappelling. Anyway, I'll see you later, *b'ezras Hashem*. Don't worry."

On that note, my son took off with his group in the minibus I'd ordered for him, heading toward Metzukeh Dragot, leveled cliffs adjacent to the Dead Sea. Cecile, their *frum* French driver, would bring them to the point of departure at the top of the mountain. He told me that no return ride was necessary as the boys could easily return home either with public transportation or by hitching rides.

The previous night, about fifteen boys had slept on our living room floor. The group needed to leave early in the morning, as the days were short, so they decided to sleep in our home. As my bedroom is off the living room, I had to navigate through a maze of soundly sleeping bodies to avoid trampling on any of them. I really didn't mind, though, since my son had set up the sleeping bags and cleaned them up afterwards.

How did our sons get involved in rappelling to begin with? Avdiel and Nechemyah always loved hiking with my husband. He taught them how to recognize the symbols on the trails and how to take all necessary precautions, including bringing a plentiful supply of drinking water, maps, flashlights, compass, and so on.

When my sons were a bit older and wanted to go hiking on their own, or with their pals, they would take the indispensable equipment and more. Hauling long ropes enabled them to get safely down mountains with less effort. My husband and I were not keen on the idea, but we didn't stop them so that they wouldn't feel they were being babied.

After numerous trials in the art of hiking with their friends, they enrolled in an official course at the Wingate Institute, a sports institute offering various courses, including mountain rappelling, to both army personnel and civilians. We reluctantly gave our permission for this course, deciding it would be better to have the boys use ropes with full knowledge of what they were doing. The cost was prohibitive, but the safety course's features compensated. Our sons had found a positive outlet for their energies during *bein hazemanim.*

After obtaining certification, Avdiel, the older of the two by a year and a half, decided to offer a course in rappelling together with his friend Yehuda to earn a little extra money.

A few weeks before the course began, he practiced with his younger sisters and brothers, going down the side of our six-story building. At first, our neighbors were quite upset, but their children, enjoying the entertainment, helped calm their fears.

One quick-tempered neighbor hissed furiously, "I'll call the police if you don't stop this immediately." One of our twins had thrown a little bike into his private garden, putting him in a disgruntled mood.

"We have a license," he was told.

Nechemyah called down to his six-year-old brother, "Moishy! You're just dangling on the rope. Put your feet on the wall for support."

Moishy hesitated, embarrassed, when he realized that all eyes were focused on him, but he kept moving steadily. When he hit the bottom, he emitted a sigh of relief and exclaimed triumphantly, "I made it!"

Saphy, next in line, took a good foothold on the wall; I watched him from the window. He gracefully maneuvered his way down the side of the building.

"Saphy, you're doing a great job!" I called out. He beamed in response.

Everyone was kept busy for a couple of hours. I ran to the window in alarm when I heard a siren-like shriek from outside. The shriek, I saw with relief, had come from my eldest daughter, who was trying out the ropes. She let out a whoop like a roller coaster rider. When she placed her feet on solid ground at the end of her journey, she grinned, pleased with her achievement.

Avdiel and Nechemyah were faced with a major problem — how to contend with their three-and-a-half-year-old sister, Rachayli. She cried and begged to go down the side of the building like the rest of her siblings.

"It's not fair! I want a turn, too!" Rachayli bawled, stamping her little feet and throwing her small arms up in frustration. Although the boys tried to charm her in various ways, they achieved nothing but frustration.

Suddenly, Nechemyah came up with an idea. Excitedly he called, "Rachayli, come quick! You're a big girl and you're ready for rappelling. I'll tie the ropes on you, so hold still."

Rachayli was ecstatic to be tied to the rappelling ropes and "flown" from our upper porch to the lower one. She was in her glory.

On the minibus, Avdiel began his first lesson, commencing with *Tefillas HaDerech*. (Yehuda related this particular incident to me later.) He added the words *"teunas derachim"* (road accidents) to the prayer, even though they are rarely added. The first puzzle piece had been put into place.

Descending into the desert was quite pleasant. Although it was already winter, the weather was very warm, in contrast to the cold mountain range from whence they'd begun their journey. The sun's rays cast prisms of light in every direction. The newly built road offered a scenic view of camels, Bedouin tents, and rolling hills of light brown rock that took on the appearance of sand from a distance. Off on the horizon, Netivot Yosef Yeshivah stood out straight and tall amongst the modest caravans surrounding it. This desert oasis of Torah learning is the only yeshivah in the area. Avdiel was proud to have been in the first graduating class of the yeshivah's exclusive high school and had gone on to learn in its post–high school program.

To avoid wasting time, Avdiel spent the bus trip presenting mountain rappelling theories and illustrating a few significant procedures. After descending from the cramped minibus, the boys stretched their legs and prepared for their final day of intense instruction and physical activity. This day would determine which of the youngsters would successfully complete the course and receive a certificate.

"Okay, everybody. Watch again as I point out the position of the person who's going to be lowered by the ropes. Let's go over the knots one more time, and then each of you will have a chance to practice before the final test. You'll need to use this information in order to follow the rules on rescuing." Avdiel's instructions were clear and precise. His friendly attitude worked wonders with the group; they adored him.

Yehuda encouraged the boys to keep on trying even if they made mistakes. Nechemyah offered demonstrations to speed up the process. Although the work was tedious, the boys didn't mind, knowing that they'd soon be receiving their coveted certificates.

As the day drew to a close, the teenagers passed their tests with flying colors and packed the ropes. The group gathered to daven *minchah* before heading back to Yerushalayim to enjoy the remainder of Chanukah.

On the joyous holiday of Chanukah, Jewish families the world over join in *pirsum hanes*. Throughout Jewish history, the people of the Book have displayed bravery in commemorating this holiday with candles or oil, remembering the miracles our people experienced in the time of the Maccabees.

Marrano Jews in Spain, during the time of the Inquisition, secretly lit candles in closets, since they could not display any connection to Judaism. Amidst the horrors of the Holocaust, there were those who risked their lives to light oil lights in moldy potatoes in order to fulfill the obligation of lighting Chanukah lights. In every generation, the Jewish people have never lost their spiritual battles, always refusing to let their oppressors take their souls.

Our strongest weapon is our faith in the One Above. All

other great nations had their downfalls and were forgotten in the annals of world history. The Jewish people, however, have survived by their faith throughout history, no matter what trials and tribulations they have undergone. The Jewish nation is invincible through its pride and faith in the Almighty. May we continue to move on with this dynamic force.

Avdiel took pride in his uncompromising efforts to fulfill the mitzvos of *bein adam laMakom* and *bein adam l'chaveiro*. His strict adherence to mitzvah performance protected him more than once. Kindling the lights and promulgating the miracle of Chanukah, in particular, had shielded him from catastrophe only the year before....

CHAPTER 3

Miracles

"Avdiel, Nechemyah, why don't the two of you get dressed for the yeshivah's Chanukah party already? It's getting late and you'll both be sorely missed if you don't show up!" I exclaimed.

"Soon, Ima. We're busy with a project now," was the indifferent response I received. Unable to distract them, even to change their clothes, I detached myself from the matter.

It was quite unusual for the two of them, who were always looking for action, to be so lackadaisical, but they never found the energy to get up and go to the party. Nechemyah, who thrives on playing drums, would have had a great opportunity to display his abilities. Avdiel, who enjoys participating in holiday festivities, showed no desire to depart from the house on that particular night. The two headed for their room to retire early, in an unusually passive state.

Only in the morning did they realize that they had, albeit unknowingly, lived through a miracle.

Avdiel's friend, Eliyahu, called while the boys were in shul. "Mrs. Jacobs, Avdiel should *bench gomel.*"

I gasped. "Eliyahu, please explain what you mean!"

Eliyahu told me, "The trailer that Avdiel slept in has burnt

to cinders, along with most of its contents. All of Avdiel's belongings have been destroyed. Radios, tape recorders, and the
like have melted —"

"I — I really thank you for notifying me, and I will certainly
pass this information on to the boys when they return from
davening," I said, a bit shaken up. "I hope — that no one was
hurt — were they?"

"*Baruch Hashem*, there wasn't anyone in the room and the
firefighters had it under control, but the damage was irrevers-
ible."

"It is truly a Chanukah miracle! Thanks — thanks again for
letting me know," I answered, still trembling.

I realized that my sons had been spared by a miracle. I
counted my blessings from the Merciful One above, Who had
prevented my sons from going to the yeshivah and safeguarding
their lives. The Guardian of Israel neither sleeps nor slumbers.

❊ ❊ ❊

At 5:10 P.M., Avdiel and the last four members of his group
stood at the roadside near Metzukeh Dragot, awaiting a ride
back to Yerushalayim. Nechemyah had left on an earlier transport with two of the more rambunctious students.

As a small green car slowed down, they noticed that it had
room for only four passengers. Three of the boys got in, and
Avdiel remained with fifteen-year-old Shai, the youngest member of his group, to await one more ride.

Ten minutes later, a shiny blue Subaru pulled up. Its driver,
who appeared to be in his early fifties, was clean shaven and exposed even white teeth behind a friendly smile. "Are you fel-
lows looking for lift to Jerusalem?"

Avdiel, overcome with exhaustion, responded, "We certainly are."

"Hop in. We'll get you there A.S.A.P.," the driver said.

A brown dog occupied the front seat, so Avdiel and Shai seated themselves in the back. As he drove, the driver told them, "I live in Kibbutz Ein Gedi."

The boys began to tell him about their experiences in the Nachal Arugot Nature Reserve. "Ein Gedi is one of my favorite hiking spots," Avdiel said heartily. He was glad to see the driver's smile through the rearview mirror.

They had been traveling for about thirty-five minutes. It was just past dusk when a small car, speeding past a large truck in the opposite lane, crossed into their lane, approaching rapidly. The driver slammed on his brakes.

Avdiel was thrown into the air. Landing face down between the two front seats, the last thing he saw before blacking out was the bright glare of four headlights.

CHAPTER 4

Lights

The night before, eight lights had burned brightly from our sparkling, sterling silver menorah. Now the festival of lights was over. The children, however, were still playing happily with their little wooden dreidel and enjoying the donuts which filled the air with such a wonderful aroma. The addition of potato latkes heightened their meal to super special.

All eyes were focused on the dreidel, dancing across the table. A joyous mood, enhanced by background music from Avraham Fried and Mordechai Ben David tapes, filled the room.

"*Gimmel*, I win!" Miryam called out as the dreidel rolled to a stop. With a smile, she took her booty and passed the dreidel to Elishama.

"*Nun*," Elishama reported. "I don't get anything, but at least I don't have to give anything."

❊　❊　❊

Yeshaya, complaining of a headache and the onset of an allergy attack, opted to retire early. "I can't seem to stop sneezing. Please excuse me; I must get some sleep," he said, his hand covering his mouth to suppress a sneeze and a yawn.

He downed his allergy pill with a generous amount of water, hoping the sneezing would cease. Unfortunately, these pills forced him into a deep sleep, but their effectiveness compensated for some excess grogginess.

"Nechemyah, where is Avdiel? Didn't he tell you he'd be coming straight home after he finished with his group?" I asked anxiously.

"Don't worry, Ima, he'll probably be home any minute. When I left him, he was waiting with Shai and a few other boys. He didn't want to leave them alone, and he said he'd be returning home as soon as they could get a ride."

At 8:45 P.M. the phone rang shrilly. I grabbed the receiver just before the answering machine beat me to it.

"I'm calling from Hadassah Hospital. Do you know an Avdiel Jacobs?" the voice on the other end asked.

My heart started to beat faster. "Yes."

"What is your relationship to Avdiel?" he continued.

"I'm — his — mother," I managed to utter, my palms growing sweaty.

"He's been in a car accident...." In the short time that elapsed before he continued, I heard my heartbeat growing louder and louder. Boom! Boom! Boom! I thought my heart would shoot right out from under my skin. My children looked at me in alarm."...but he's all right. He's here next to me, waiting to talk to you."

I held onto the edge of the table near me. At last I heard my son's strained voice, "Eee-Eee-Im-a, Ima, Ahm aw right."

Had the nurse presented the facts in the reverse order, notifying me that my son was all right and then giving the news that he'd been in an accident, I would have been spared the near heart attack.

A thousand questions ran through my mind. *My dear Avdiel Yitzchak, what are you feeling now? Are you in a lot of pain, my sweet son? What exactly happened? Were you frightened?* I knew that with Hashem's help all would turn out well in the end, and our family's faith in HaKadosh Baruch Hu would only be strengthened.

Landing back on planet earth, I realized that the male nurse had been talking and I hadn't been listening. "Mrs. Jacobs, are you there?"

"Yes, I'm here," I whispered.

"Either you or your husband will have to come down to stay with Avdiel, as he is in the trauma ward."

With shaking legs, I shuffled over to the bedroom to wake my slumbering husband. On the way, I was bombarded with questions from my clan.

"Ima, what happened to Avdiel?" asked Elishama in a fearful voice.

"He's been in a car accident. I don't know all the details, darling," I sighed, my head still reeling.

"Avdiel's been in a car accident?" Nechemyah repeated. He reached up to the shelf, pulled out a *Sefer Tehillim* and opened it. Some of the other children followed suit.

I jumped as the phone jangled again. It was my mother-in-law. I didn't want her to detect fear in my voice, so after a brief "Hello, Mom," I handed the receiver to Miryam, telling her to make conversation with Bubby so I could go wake her father. I motioned to her, with a finger pressed to my lips, not to let Bubby know anything about the situation; fortunately, she understood.

I proceeded to the bedroom and called my husband's name gently to wake him. "What's the matter? I need more sleep," he murmured.

"Yeshaya, I'm really sorry to have to disturb you, but you need to get up now to go to the hospital. Avdiel's okay...but he's been in a severe car crash. One of us has to remain with him." Tears welled up in my eyes.

Pulling himself up in bed, Yeshaya just stared at me, not saying a word. It wasn't like him not to respond. He seemed to be in a different world. He must have been under the influence of the allergy pill he'd taken.

"Abba, Bubby's on the phone," Miryam called out, when she saw her father moving about the room.

He took the receiver in his clammy hand, said a few words out of respect for his mother, and then proceeded to get dressed without saying anything to me. Had I done or said something wrong? He grabbed his coat, his car keys, and a few coins. Out the door he went, without even a good-bye to me. Dismayed by his strange behavior, I tried my best to give him the benefit of the doubt. Perhaps his confusion was caused by the shocking news.

Remembering my responsibilities as a mother, I knew I had to stay in control during the crisis. I said *Tehillim* with the children and then put them to bed, worrying all the while about my son.

Until I heard from Yeshaya, I knew it would be impossible for me to even attempt going to sleep. What was expected of me now? What was the proper action to take?

Prayer — before anything else, my heartfelt *tefillah* was required.

My tears flowed unchecked; I lifted my eyes in prayer to the Ribbono shel Olam. "HaKadosh Baruch Hu, please let my son, Avdiel Yitzchak ben Rivkah Leah, fully recuperate. He is a dedicated *ben Torah* and will continue to serve You sincerely. Please let his mind and all of his limbs remain unharmed and allow them to continue functioning properly! Forgive me for any sin I may have committed against You, and may any *zechus* I have earned go toward Avdiel's complete recovery. Remember Your promise to our people — if one performs the mitzvah of *kibbud av va'eim*, he is rewarded with a long life. Apply this to my son, in this world as well as in the next, as his parental respect always goes beyond the letter of the law." I closed my eyes, sighed, and waited.

My eyelids began to droop and I had nearly fallen asleep when I heard the loud ring of the phone.

"Rivkah, it's me, Yeshaya. I'll be staying here for the night with Avdiel. He is still in the trauma ward, but he seems to be slowly coming out of it and getting better."

"I've been anxiously waiting for your call. I'm so worried about Avdiel's condition. What exactly happened? How did —?"

"My dear Rivkah, Avdiel is, *baruch Hashem*, all right. He had to have some stitches in his head and he has a broken arm, but otherwise he's doing well. I apologize about the way I acted earlier. I'll be home in the morning and I'll clarify everything then. In the meanwhile, please try to get some sleep."

Unable to banish thoughts of the accident, I put forth an additional urgent plea. "Dear God, please allow the light of Chanukah to continue to shine upon our house, our family, and the Jewish nation."

CHAPTER 5

Scene of the Accident

At 5:45 P.M., immediately after the head-on collision occurred, the car tumbled down the side of the mountain. Turning its passengers upside down more than once, it finally landed right side up.

Shai, the only person in the car to have remained conscious, was in a state of shock. Frightened out of his wits, he watched the dog jump out the front window, barking loudly. Shai touched Avdiel, shaking him, but received no response. He couldn't get near enough to the driver to see what had happened to him. The door near him was jammed shut, and when he tried to open the window, it also proved to be stuck. Shai sat and waited, feeling helpless.

An army jeep, which had been located approximately three minutes from the scene of the accident, arrived promptly. Moving toward the car, one of the soldiers in the jeep wired the ambulance, demanding assistance.

"Emergency! Nearest ambulance must get to the scene of an accident ten kilometers south of Mitzpeh Yericho. Over," he shouted into the mouthpiece.

Fortunately, the ambulance driver and his crew resided less than a ten-minute drive away. While awaiting their arrival, the soldiers pried open the car doors, so that the emergency crew could extract the victims speedily.

Before long, the ambulance arrived, its siren blaring. The driver and Avdiel were each lifted gently onto stretchers; Shai walked into the ambulance on his own.

"Gently! Can't take any chance with broken limbs!" the head of the ambulance crew directed the others. "Slowly move him onto the stretcher. That's it. Carry him up and get an IV started at once. You two take care of the next one and administer IV instantly. No time to lose here. We have to transport the victims straightaway to the hospital emergency room. There's no way of knowing precisely how much blood's been lost."

Both the driver and Avdiel were unconscious. Avdiel's face and head were covered with blood. One of the medics tending him tried to locate the source of the bleeding, covering it with swathes of bandages to help it to cease. He then attempted to cut the blue down coat Avdiel was wearing.

Avdiel stirred and mumbled, "Don't cut the coat! It will send feathers flying all over."

The medic couldn't believe his ears. Shortly after Avdiel fell back into an unconscious state, and the medic proceeded to care for him without destroying the coat. Little did he know that the coat belonged to Avdiel's brother. A caring and responsible individual, Avdiel had been stirred to consciousness in order to protect his brother's belongings.

The ambulance driver, a member of the *yishuv* of Mitzpeh Yericho, had recognized Avdiel's name and picture on his *teudat zehut* (identity card). He immediately notified the yeshivah so that the *bachurim* could say *Tehillim* for him.

A lone screaming siren echoed in the night; the white ambulance, its red light illuminating the dark night like a ball of fire, sped to Hadassah Ein Kerem hospital.

Upon arrival at the emergency ward, each of the victims was cared for according to his needs. The driver was wheeled into the operating room so his broken ribs and teeth could be attended to. Avdiel 's head was sutured with about twenty stitches; a cast was fitted around his broken right arm. He was then moved to the trauma ward, where he drifted in and out of consciousness while he waited for a family member to arrive. Shai was treated for shock while his family in Be'er Sheva was notified.

Receiving the summons from the hospital, Shai's parents got into their car immediately and headed up to Jerusalem. Turning on the radio, they listened to the news broadcast and discovered that a car accident had occurred not far from Mitzpeh Yericho, killing all of its victims. Shai's mother went in a stupor. When they entered the hospital, she fainted right in front of the nurses.

Yes, there had been an accident on the same road earlier that day. Those people had, tragically, lost their lives. It was a true miracle that all three inhabitants of the blue Subaru had been spared. More pieces of the Master of the Universe's giant puzzle were put into place.

While sleep eluded me, I drifted off to the past, remembering Avdiel's birth.

CHAPTER 6

Beginnings

It was Rosh HaShanah, 1976. Davening *Shemoneh Esrei* in shul, I experienced the onset of labor. We were living in Silver Spring, Maryland, at the time, staying with my in-laws until housing became available.

The minute I finished my *tefillah*, I decided to go home for a nap. I told my mother-in-law, who was beside me in shul, "Mom, I'm going home for a little bit to catch a few winks. I'm utterly exhausted." I didn't mention the contractions, so she wouldn't worry about me.

Nodding, she whispered, "Go ahead, honey. I'll come and check on you later."

Although I was still feeling infrequent labor pains, I took my one-and-a-half-year-old daughter with me to my in-laws' house around the corner from the shul, walking as steadily as possible. Settling her into her crib for a nap, I went to my room for my sorely needed repose.

❋ ❋ ❋

My husband was teaching in the school that he had attended sixteen years before. His colleagues, his former rebbes, were proud of his accomplishments. He had been a mischievous pupil, with lots of energy, and he started teaching with unbridled enthusiasm. Students flocked to his classes, never missing a single lesson. Yeshaya captivated them with his charismatic ways and exciting stories.

One of his classes was a group of disinterested, indifferent boys. When my husband was ill, he asked me to substitute. I walked into the classroom fearfully and was pleasantly surprised when the ruffians behaved like perfect angels.

After class one of them approached me. "You know, Mrs. J., if any other substitute would have been here today, we'd have caused a big ruckus, but we were on our best behavior for you." He shifted his weight from one leg to the other and continued, "It's because Rabbi J. really cares about us. When we learned about the court system in the Gemara, he took us on a class trip to the judiciary and we performed a play on the topic. No other teacher ever did such a thing! They never found our class worthy of going on an outing.

"He treats us with respect and dignity, so how can we not respect and love him? If we pay attention to his lessons, he treats us to one of his fantastic tales. When he left class yesterday, he was right in the middle of a great story and we want to hear the rest of it. Please be sure to tell him how well we behaved for you. Okay?"

"Okay!" I answered, amazed, just beginning to understand my husband's talents.

(Later, many of these students straightened out and went on to learn in post–high school yeshivos. For years hence, mothers would call to tell us about the positive influence my husband had had on their sons.)

❖   ❖   ❖

About an hour later, I vaguely heard crying coming from

the next room, but I was too tired to move. I faintly heard footsteps in the background, followed by the sobs subsiding. Rescued by her *bubby*, my daughter was taken out of her crib and given some lunch. I fell back asleep, soon to be awakened by an affectionate little girl climbing up onto my bed.

That evening, during the festive Rosh HaShanah meal, I felt the contractions gaining a powerful edge over me. When they started coming six minutes apart, my husband and I decided that it was time to break the news to my in-laws.

"Mom, Dad, Rivky's in labor, and we'll be going to the hospital soon," Yeshaya announced.

His mother, who had been busy in the kitchen, grabbed the counter behind her so as not to lose her balance. "For someone in labor, you sure are taking this quite calmly!"

"It's okay, Mom. We'll call the doctor right away; Rivkah will heed his advice."

Still panicky, she ran to confer with my father-in-law. "Abe! Rivky's going to have the baby!"

My father-in-law replied, "Sadye, what do you want me to do?" Turning in my direction, he ordered, "Call the taxi already and go!"

Although it was Rosh HaShanah, I was permitted to use the telephone to notify the doctor, since it was a case of *pikuach nefesh*. Then I packed the necessities and my husband called a taxi. The holiday had fallen on Shabbos and Sunday, and I was happy that it was now after nightfall, permitting us to carry the shofar to the hospital, which is allowed only on *yom tov*, not on Shabbos.

The taxi arrived. My father-in-law confounded the driver by telling him, "My daughter-in-law is in labor. Drive quickly to get her to the hospital in a hurry; drive slowly, so nothing will happen to her or the unborn child."

We made it to the George Washington University Hospital in less than an hour. At 3:00 A.M. a healthy baby boy was born into the Jacobs family. He didn't cry; he lifted up his tiny head, moving it back and forth, until I was allowed to nurse him, right on the delivery table.

Our newborn infant weighed seven pounds, four ounces. He had delicate features and a little bit of blonde hair. To me, he was the sweetest little baby in the world.

Because it was the second day of Rosh HaShanah, I knew it would still be almost another fifteen hours until we could let both sets of parents know about their new grandson. Yeshaya went to Georgetown, walking distance from the G. W. Hospital, to daven *shacharis*. I was wheeled into a room on the maternity ward.

I was fairly uncomfortable, since I could not adjust my electronically adjusting bed on *yom tov*. When the nurse changed my bed's position in order to help me comfortably nurse my newborn, I couldn't even ask her to place it back into its original position. I felt like a trapped animal, confined in a cage.

My rest was disturbed further by my roommate's rented television, located directly above my bed. She was totally absorbed by the screen, barely noticing me.

When the nurse entered carrying our breakfast platters, I noticed that my tray looked exactly like my roommate's. I'd ordered a strictly kosher meal, and I felt uncomfortable when I saw that we'd both received the same food: a scrambled egg, juice, butter, jelly, salad, tea, and cottage cheese. I asked the nurse, "Is this a kosher tray?"

Her response was, "No, ma'am, you get kosher meals only for dinner."

"So what am I supposed to do for breakfast and lunch?" I asked indignantly.

"It's only dairy. There's no meat or anything on the tray. Vegetarian!"

How could she know that nonkosher cottage cheese contains gelatin made from pig's feet? I was considered a sick person whose life is in danger since I was during the first three days after childbirth, but I wasn't ready to sacrifice the *kedushah* of the day with *treif* food.

I ate minimally — only the items that were not cooked.

Frustrated by the dilemma, I patiently awaited the nurse's return. I wanted to dispose of the meal tray as soon as possible, and I still didn't know how to resolve the quandary of the television. At home we didn't even own a television, and *frum* people who did would never dream of turning it on on Rosh HaShanah, the holy Day of Judgment. My eyes vacillated between the television and the woman occupying the adjacent bed. I knew that one of us had to go — it was either the TV or me.

In about ten minutes, the nurse approached.

"Nurse! I need help urgently."

"What can I do for you, young lady?" she responded, smiling. "Do you need some help with the baby?"

"No, it's like this." I motioned for her to move a bit closer so that I could converse with her quietly. She bent down to listen. "I am Jewish, and today is our Jewish New Year; hence, I am not permitted to watch television. I would like to be switched to another room. Would you be so kind as to help me?"

"I'll see what I can do," she responded, somewhat bemused.

Before long I was moved into a large room, empty of occupants. Exhilarated to be alone, I finally fell asleep.

Upon his return, Yeshaya approached the nursing station to ask if he could blow the ram's horn for his wife, as it was the Jewish New Year. He was granted permission. As I had been moved to a private room, he was able to blow the entire one hundred blasts for me, while not a person stirred. When he finished, I felt like a new person.

When *yom tov* was over the phone rang. It was my mother-in-law. "Yes, Mom, you've merited a wonderful healthy new grandson, as cute as he can be."

"Oh, Rivky, it's so exciting! Who does he look like? I can't wait to see him." she gushed.

"I think he looks like a Crystal, but it's too early to tell."

"We'll bring over some snacks and the items you couldn't bring on Yom Tov."

"I could really use extra food — they only supply me with kosher food once a day."

"Really!"

Floating on cloud nine, I phoned Ohio. "Hi, Mom. Please put Dad on the other line; I want to share some terrific news with both of you.... Dad, are you there? You are now the proud grandparents of a delightful new *yingele*."

"That's wonderful!" My parents were thrilled about the arrival of their first grandson, who gave *nachas* to all of us.

❉   ❉   ❉

On the eighth day of my son's life, the bris was held in the shul near my in-laws' home. My parents drove in from Cleveland to share this joyous occasion.

"...and his name shall be called in the nation of Israel Avdiel Yitzchak."

How did we choose his name? A child born on Rosh HaShanah is extremely special. *Akeidas Yitzchak* is read on this holiday, portraying the genuine devotion of both Avraham Avinu and Yitzchak. Both were ready to make the complete and ultimate sacrifice to HaKadosh Baruch Hu. Yitzchak Avinu proved to be a true servant of Hashem. Yeshaya's brother and grandfather (*zichronam livrachah*) were also named Yitzchak. The name *Avdiel* means a "servant of God." Avdiel was from the tribe of Gad, which was composed of mighty warriors. We hoped that our son would become a soldier in the Almighty's great army. Just as Yitzchak Avinu was a soldier of Hashem, it was our desire that our son be a faithful servant of HaKadosh Baruch Hu. Hence, the name Avdiel Yitzchak was chosen.

Avdiel was a clever child. At sixteen months, on our way to the shopping center, he'd point to the various cars. "This is a red car. This is a green car. That is a blue car."

When he was two and a half, Avdiel's long blonde ponytail made him look like a becoming, petite girl. However, in every respect, he played like a boy. My mother-in-law labeled him her sunshine, putting a framed picture of him next to her bed.

I still remember the first time that we visited my friend Bryna, whose firstborn had been a boy. Up until that time, we hadn't thought of buying Avdiel matchbox cars or any other specifically "male" toys. Our only toys were blocks and dolls, as our firstborn was a girl.

My friend's son, Yossie, was playing with his toy train and cars. Avdiel stood transfixed, enthralled by the scene. Moving closer, he seated himself beside the locomotives, wagons, and cars and began to play, oblivious to everything else. I acknowledged the fact that the time had come to purchase cars for our toy collection.

My daughter, barely glancing at the car display, continued to Bryna's daughter's room, where the collection of toy kitchen equipment and dolls held her attention. The two children had certainly disproved the theories that a child is taught to behave as a boy or girl. It was obvious that it was an inborn instinct.

Men and women were given different characteristics, which I could see clearly when I watched my children playing.

By the time Avdiel was almost three, in July of 1979, we came on aliyah. Along with the rest of the family, he was confronted with many challenges. As we boarded the plane in New York, he held on tightly to his little blue case of matchbox cars, which he refused to pack in our luggage lest they get lost. They served as his security.

Avdiel's small suitcase accompanied him a long route, from the airport to Moshav Mevo Charon (a *moshav shitufi*), and even into the classroom.

Learning Hebrew and adapting to Israeli society was no easy feat. It caused many frustrations for him, his sister, and his brother. On various occasions he'd let out his anger at the "foreign country"; however, once he'd mastered the language, he began to make friends and adapted to all the nuances of Israeli culture.

July, 1986

Avdiel was growing up amongst the rolling hills and plains of the beautiful country of Eretz Yisrael. From a very young age, he enjoyed mountain climbing and hiking. Where else in the world can one experience snow in Jerusalem, and merely half an hour's ride away take a pleasant swim in the Dead Sea (with a *mechitzah* in the water)? Exploring, scaling foothills, running, and strolling all became a part of Avdiel's life. No matter where we were living at the time (and we've had to move frequently), he was always able to find solace in his agility and ability to roam freely in his own land.

Promised to the Jewish people from the time of Avraham Avinu, this beautiful country, flowing with milk and honey, has provided us with the opportunity to perform many mitzvos. Among the 613 mitzvos that are incumbent on a Jew, many can be fulfilled only in Eretz Yisrael. Special *berachos* are said on the fruits of Israel. *Terumah, ma'asros,* and *shemittah* only apply to the produce of the Land of Israel. In addition, we are taught, "There is no Torah like the Torah of Eretz Yisrael."

Avdiel thrived on the mitzvos of Eretz Yisrael, and his Torah learning progressed rapidly. He had skills that far surpassed what he would have had if we'd remained in the United States.

On Rosh Hashanah, 1989, at the age of thirteen, Avdiel reached Jewish manhood. Yeshaya asked the *rosh yeshivah* if Avdiel would be entitled to have an *aliyah* on his birthday, the second day of Rosh HaShanah. The answer was in the affirmative.

Generally, only important, well-respected members of the community are called up to the Torah on Rosh HaShanah. Suddenly, a young boy's loud, clear, sweet voice could be heard reciting the *berachah*. My husband and I, filled with pride, were thankful to have been blessed with a son whose day of birth coincided with Rosh HaShanah.

The Shabbos that followed, Avdiel read the parashah of *Ha'azinu* from the Torah. Again we overflowed with joy, listening to our son *leining*.

On Sukkos, we hosted a *seudah* in the sukkah of the Beit El yeshivah. Avdiel looked so handsome in his new navy blue suit as he gave his speech like a noble, royal servant of the Almighty. The festivities included singing and dancing, accompanied by Akiva Margaliot and his organ. My beaming parents were thrilled to attend the affair, having journeyed to Israel from Cleveland, Ohio.

Coming out of my trance, I asked the Almighty to assist me in another *seudah*, that of *hoda'ah*. "Please, Hashem, return my son to me, safe, sound, and complete; physically, mentally, and spiritually. Enable me, together with my husband, to partake in a *seudas hoda'ah* for Avdiel Yitzchak ben Rivkah Leah."

Closing my eyes, I drifted back to July 1990.

Avdiel's next significant milestone in life was his acceptance to the yeshivah of Netivot Yosef. In his four years there, he had the opportunity to grow in his *yiras Shamayim*, fully blossoming into manhood. The challenge to learn a *daf* of Gemara daily was met with success.

He lived in a small trailer (containing a bedroom, shower, and a small study area) with meager *gashmius*, but his *ruchnius* was abundant. The desert heat was overbearing at times, but the *beis midrash* was equipped with a desert cooler (later replaced by an air conditioner), making the facility a pleasant place for learning. A full schedule, including a secular studies program, demanded double work, but most of the students thrived.

During *bein hazemanim*, Avdiel would always take to the road with his hiking skills. Second to his love for learning Torah was his love for mountain rappelling and climbing. This eventually led him to the official rappelling course at the Wingate Institute.

Exhausted, I fell into a deep sleep.

CHAPTER 7

The Dream

Yeshaya's arrival home, the morning after the accident, was accompanied by the children's anxious questions.

"Abba, is Avdiel going to be all right?"

"Will Hashem let him live?"

"When is he coming home?"

The questions were coming faster than the answers could be provided. My husband explained the situation in a way that they could grasp it.

"How was your night? How did Avdiel look?" I asked when the children had gone out to play.

"I managed to sleep a little, but noisy apparatus kept me up most of the time. Avdiel wasn't exactly the most pleasant to look at, but *b'ezras Hashem* he will recover."

"When do you think he'll be released?"

"Tomorrow morning, *b'ezras Hashem*. His friends are visiting with him now. Yehuda phoned to ask if there was anything that Avdiel needed, and he brought many of his fellow yeshivah friends to visit. Rav Sabato had gathered the students together to recite *Tehillim* as soon as they'd received the news about the accident. Do you know what? The ambulance driver was from Mitzpeh Yericho and wasted no time in notifying the yeshivah immediately."

"Unbelievable! Go on." I thought about the great puzzle that Hashem has in His possession, and how every once in a while we can see how the pieces fit in. Sometimes it is evident, and other times not. In this particular case it was apparent.

"I really apologize for my behavior last night, but...."

"No, dear, you don't have to apologize," I interrupted. "You were under stress; I understood."

"No, please let me explain. When you woke me up, I couldn't speak to you because I had just had a dream about the accident!"

"You're kidding!"

"Yes, I dreamt that Avdiel was in a car accident and his right arm flew up in the air and came back down again. It turned out that his right arm was broken! After being awoken from this vivid nightmare, hearing you tell me that I have to go to the hospital because Avdiel had just been in a car accident, I couldn't speak. I was stupefied."

"You know, Yeshaya, when I attended Rav Leff's lectures on the *neshamah* he once told us how a *neshamah* can occasionally hook up to another *neshamah* that it is close to in a dream." I shook my head in amazement, looking at my husband with admiration. "I'm not exactly sure how it works, but we can contact the tape library if we want to hear all the details.... But now I just hope that Avdiel will recover completely, with no scars or lasting damage from the accident."

"The doctors said that his mind was, *baruch Hashem*, not affected by the accident," Yeshaya assured me. "He had trouble talking last night because his jaw had been dislocated, but the doctors have readjusted it and it should heal without difficulty."

"How about the driver and Shai?"

"The driver lost his two front teeth and will eventually need implants, and he broke a few ribs. I think he received the worst of the impact. Shai went into shock, but he's already recovered.

There was also a bit of a scare with his mother, who fainted upon arrival at the hospital. I'll tell you the rest of the story later."

The next morning, Avdiel, still clothed in the blue and white striped hospital robe, somehow managed to maneuver into our van. My husband tried to make him as comfortable as possible for the drive home.

CHAPTER 8

Recovery

Avdiel's arrival brought great excitement to the Jacobs household. He actually arrived at a quieter time of the morning and had some time to rest before his younger siblings came home from school. His right arm was bound in a white plaster cast which begged for autographs, while his head was swathed in bandages that covered most of his blonde hair, but his blue eyes shone brightly as he recited *Tehillim* and expressed his gratitude to Hashem for emerging alive from the terrible accident.

Avdiel's arm would need at least six weeks in the cast, but the stitches in his head could be extracted within about a week. It was a miracle that he didn't have any other injuries; those that he had sustained could be considered minimal, considering the head-on collision he'd experienced.

Time passed rather slowly for Avdiel, a normally active nineteen-year-old. His friends' visits were a welcome distraction. Various classmates and acquaintances spent their afternoons in our apartment. The accident stayed in Avdiel's mind for a very long time, and he reenacted the scene whenever he spoke about it with his friends. He put a strong emphasis on his being alive due to a miracle, reiterating his thankfulness to HaKadosh Baruch Hu.

Nechemyah and Yehuda went to retrieve Avdiel's belongings from the vehicle. They were quite frightened when they saw the wrecked car, which had been almost completely destroyed. Was it from this wreckage that their brother and friend had survived — this car (or what was left of it)? Yehuda recalled Avdiel's inclusion of the words *"teunas derachim"* in his recital of *Tefillas HaDerech* the morning of the accident.

After salvaging the remains of Avdiel's belongings, the boys couldn't help discussing the Divine intervention that had taken place.

Most miracles that the Almighty performs are compatible with nature. If we are cognizant of our surroundings, we can see that miracles are being performed daily. Crossing the street and not being hit by an oncoming car is an act of Hashem's mercy. If the brakes suddenly stop working, the driver is not alert, or rain causes excessive slipperiness, the approaching vehicle can easily hit whoever, or whatever, happens to be in the way. With His abundance of everlasting mercy, our Creator prevents such calamities almost all the time. How often do we take our lives and all the events that occur on any given day for granted? If we would just take the time, on a daily basis, to be more appreciative of all the daily miracles performed, we would be more attuned to the *hashgachah peratis* in the world.

A few weeks passed and Avdiel was finally ready to return to his studies in the yeshivah. We notified Rav Sabato, his *rosh yeshivah*, of our desire to prepare a *seudas hoda'ah* for our family members and the *yeshivah bachurim*. We made arrangements for a special lunch for the class.

Escorted into the classroom on the appointed day, we took our seats at a lovingly set table boasting an array of Israeli-style salads. Extra sodas, cakes, and goodies had to be ordered for the occasion. Aside from a donation to the yeshivah, we planned to pick up the tab for the extras.

Yeshaya, the first speaker, focused on our gratitude to Hashem for returning our son — complete in mind and body.

Rav Sabato spoke next, giving inspiring *divrei Torah*. He sent chills down my spine when he gazed at Avdiel and concluded, "You've used up all of your *zechuyos*. You will now have to start over again, like a newborn baby."

I blinked back my tears, indebted to the Almighty for my son — the best gift I ever received.

After years of accumulating mitzvos, Avdiel's score had been, in a figurative sense, brought to zero. He would now have to face the challenge of starting over. I didn't doubt his undertaking of this new responsibility. His constant labor in fulfilling the mitzvah of honoring his parents was repaid by the Ribbono shel Olam in this world (and, *b'ezras Hashem*, his share in the World to Come would be held off until 120).

As stated in the Torah, the reward for one who observes the commandment of honoring his parents is an extension of days, and our family was fortunate to receive this reward.

To conclude the *seudah* we offered our sincere thanks to the Ribbono shel Olam for His everlasting mercy in saving Avdiel Yitzchak's life.

For the moment, all the puzzle pieces were firmly in place.

Book Three

MY FATHER'S
INNER
STRENGTH

CHAPTER 1

The Question

Late Sunday afternoon, March 9, 1997

My brother's voice came over the receiver. "Laibel here. Sorah and I just saw Dad, and he welcomed us sitting up in his wheelchair. He said emphatically, 'Rivkah is supposed to be here.' I told him that you're in Israel, but he insisted, 'She should be here.'

"Rabbi Schur asked us to make an emergency flight from Denver to Cleveland, as Dad's health was rapidly declining," Laibel continued. "When I asked Dad what he was doing down in the lobby, he just said, 'I came to greet you.' Frankly, I was quite stunned to see him. Can you imagine? We had been told the situation is extremely critical, and there he was waiting for us!

"Rivkah, he really wants to see you. What do you think? Would it be feasible for you to make the trip in?"

"Laibel," I answered, without hesitation, "I'll order a round-trip ticket from Israel to Cleveland for Thursday, since it will take me a few days to get organized. God willing, I'll be granted another chance to see Dad."

Thoughts were gyrating in my head like a spinning top.

Speculations as to what lay ahead of me in the coming days filled my mind. Would I have another chance to behold my Dad and spend some time with him? The answer would be up to the Almighty.

I needed to organize my time. I thought to myself, *Let's see. The following list is high priority: purchase airline tickets, shop for convenience foods, and arrange places for the children to go after school. As soon as Yeshaya comes home, I'll discuss the remainder of the details with him, and we'll consider how to proceed further. I'll make a list of instructions and a chart of chores with important reminders for all family members. Running a household without me won't be easy. Everyone in the family depends on me, and in order to make a journey of this nature, I need to have everything ready.*

I felt that it was my duty, as a daughter, to do everything conceivable to achieve my father's request, provided that my spouse had no objections. A married woman's first obligation is to her husband, but I was quite sure that there would be no objections.

My father had requested that I come again. He really wanted me to be with him.

CHAPTER 2

Bringing the Mountain

Late January, 1997

Six weeks earlier my brother Laibel had called to let me know the statistics and how imperative it was for me to come immediately. According to the doctors, my father's time in this world was quite limited.

I valued the precious time I had left and worked feverishly to achieve my goals. When I asked my oldest daughter to join me in flying to the States to see Saba, she immediately responded affirmatively and her husband seconded the motion. This was our opportunity to let my father see his only great-grandson, and we didn't want to miss it.

Within twenty-four hours my daughter, my grandson, and I headed down the runway. With seat belts fastened, we looked out the small window at the houses that appeared tinier and tinier, becoming little dots and squares on an exquisitely woven patchwork quilt as our plane accelerated into the vast blue expanse of sky.

When we landed, we had to pass through customs. That was when our troubles began. Rather than applying for an American passport, which would take too much time, we requested a visa for my sweet, brown-eyed little grandson.

The INS agent, a stout fellow with a blue and gold uniform that barely covered his protruding belly, cast a wary look at us. Glancing down at our passports, he spoke gruffly, in a heavy Brooklyn accent. "It's not possible for the kid to be an Israeli citizen and not an American one!" His salt and pepper mustache matched his hair, framing a round red face; his crimson cheeks seemed to be turning redder by the minute.

I answered, "But, sir, his father is an Israeli."

He drew himself up to his full height and furiously bore his eyes into mine. "Listen, lady! His mother, here, is American. You are the kid's grandmother, and you're an American citizen. So he has to be an American citizen, too!"

He simply couldn't figure out why the baby, whose mother and grandmother were holding valid American passports, came with an Israeli visa.

My daughter nervously pushed the loose strands of her strawberry blonde *sheitel* off her brow and looked at me with a "what now?" expression on her face.

I persisted anxiously, "When we received the news of my father's precarious condition, we had to move at full speed and couldn't be bogged down with details like a passport, which could take up to a week to receive. There was simply no time to apply for an American passport."

The agent, shaking his weary head, muttered, "Carry on."

Taking in a full breath and standing on my tiptoes to appear a bit taller, I said, "Mister, it is a matter of life and death! We must catch the plane to Cleveland now!"

He appeared ready to relent. "My father's life is hanging by a thread," I added for good measure, holding my breath.

On this note, he finally capitulated. Peering over his reading spectacles, he huffed, "Okay, ladies. Take the baby on through. But next time, make sure he has his American passport!"

The last leg of our journey proved uneventful, and we were grateful for our safe arrival in Cleveland. By the time we had reached our destination, we were absolutely fatigued.

Laibel, who had flown in just a few days earlier, met us at the airport. Some stubble on his chin was the result of a few days without a shave. Balancing his job, his family, and the regular trips from Denver to Cleveland was more than the average person could manage; however, Laibel was not one to buckle under these pressures. His superb quality of making honoring his parents a priority was not to be underestimated.

"It's great to see all of you. You can't imagine how much Dad will appreciate this visit!" Stroking the baby's cheek, Laibel added, "He'll perk up when he sets his eyes on this little one."

We decided to go straight to the hospital in order not to waste any time, even though we were almost too tired to move. After coming all this way, it would be ludicrous to miss the opportunity to see Dad.

Laibel picked Mom up along the way. "Mom, it's so wonderful to see you again!" I said, hugging her.

"It's great to see all of you, too," Mom responded enthusiastically. She was eager to talk, but I asked if we could push off the chatting time until the morning, since we were so tired.

"That's fine," Mom said, though her voice expressed some disappointment.

Laibel drove us right up to the hospital entrance, so we wouldn't have to stay out in the subzero temperature for long. We emerged into the howling wind and walked quickly to the entrance, trying to keep the baby as warm as possible.

Inside, I felt a rush of hot air against my face. We boarded a stuffy elevator, which smelled of ethanol, and advanced toward Dad's room.

I walked ahead of the others, in order to prepare my father for the surprise visit. As I hurried down the corridor, images danced before my eyes: the plain walls, the bare furniture, and the uniformly painted doors. Each room contained its own melancholy story, unknown to any newspaper columnist.

Finally, I reached my father's room. I found myself standing silently near the door, peeking in. It had been about two and a half years since I'd seen my father last. Yes, the aging process had begun to set in. The white hospital gown hung loosely around him. He'd lost some weight, though not much. His thin brown hair, covering most of the surface of his bald spot, had turned gray at the temples. His bright blue eyes seemed a bit watery, and his face had a sallow tinge to it. Resting my eyes on his wrinkled, slightly shriveled hands, I realized how tired and worn out Dad looked, almost like a weeping willow tree. Morphine was keeping the edge off my father's excruciating pain. I wanted to cry out, to help in whatever way I could; but help could only come from Above. My task was to offer him the encouragement and support he needed.

Dad had been through a number of ordeals, but he always proved to be a fighter. With Hashem's help, he would pull through, against all odds, with his tremendous desire to live.

The year before, Dad had come down with a severe case of pneumonia and had to be hospitalized in an intensive care ward for twelve days. The doctors were amazed that he pulled through. Indeed, it was a miracle. Dad's life seemed like that of a cat with nine lives. His superb affinity to the mitzvah of honoring his parents clearly added years to his life. Take, for example, an incident that occurred ten years prior to his illness:

It was January, 1987. One very icy winter morning, when my father was driving his Chevy to work, his car slid over a slippery ice patch. He'd been coasting down Noble Road toward the main intersection of Monticello Boulevard when the vehicle swerved, spun around, and smashed violently into a tree, literally cutting the car in half.

When the policeman arrived at the scene of the accident, he exclaimed, "No one could have come out of this alive!" He then noticed my father, nearly unscathed, with merely a scratch or two, leaning against one half of the car. Releasing a whistle, the police officer admitted, "I think I just witnessed a miracle."

❋　❋　❋

In January, 1997, I straightened my blouse and gently knocked on the wide door. I mustered a smile. "Daddy! How are you?"

Inclining his head toward me in his congenial manner, he returned the smile. "Doll face! It's great to see you! You look terrific!"

I thought to myself that he didn't look so terrific. Tubes in his nose kept the oxygen flowing into his nostrils. The food on his plate looked unpalatable, resembling baby food, unfit for my kingly father. Dad, who had long ago lifted us up in the air to play "out the window" — a game involving a toss up in the air, followed by a throw over his shoulder — seemed so sedentary now.

Giving him a peck on the cheek, I said softly, trying to sound cheerful, "Daddy, I have another surprise for you. I brought not only your granddaughter, but your great-grandson."

"You're fantastic! If you can't go to the mountain, you bring the mountain to you," he rejoined happily. He still retained his sense of humor.

Just then the rest of the family entered, and Dad became ecstatic. "Look at this little guy! He's really something." Gingerly, he held his great-grandson on his lap. As the baby bounced on him, I could detect my father's face cringing with pain, but he didn't allow it to distract him from this pleasurable moment. His beaming smile said it all. It was worth every penny and every minute of lost sleep to share this precious moment.

Both my daughter and I had to turn our faces away and blink back the tears. She had been a little girl herself not so long ago, basking in the attention of her Saba: sitting on his lap and bouncing up and down and laughing with him at his funny jokes.

We remained with him for close to half an hour. The time was well spent, but my daughter and I were on the verge of collapse from fatigue. "Dad, *b'ezras Hashem*, we'll be back to see you tomorrow. The baby's had a rough trip. Love you loads, and please, try to get some rest."

"Thanks, doll face, it means a lot to me that you came!" Tears glittered in Dad's eyes. Each one of us gave him a gentle hug and kiss before departing.

Approaching my parents' home brought back so many memories. I remembered trudging to school in knee-deep snow, the type that crunched like cookies underfoot. Looking around me, I noticed the neatly plowed streets and the snowbanks along the sides of the road. The streetlights glowed while the powdery flakes twinkled in front of them, falling to the cotton-layered ground.

Although I am proud to have made my own home in Israel, I couldn't help my reminiscing, recalling how Laibel and I used to haul our sleds out of the garage. Dad loved to join us when we built snowmen and had snowball fights.

In Cane Park I huffed and puffed. "Laibel, we made it! Just take a look at this steep hill. I can't wait to slide down. It's so exciting!" All around us there were throngs of children who couldn't resist the opportune weather, taking advantage of the glistening snow-laden hill of Cane Park. It beckoned us to take the plunge and glide down into its depths.

"Let's grab a spot quick before there isn't any room left to move," Laibel said.

On both sides of the hill stood the towering evergreens, their roots anchored securely in the ground while their glistening, pearly white peaks reached up to the sky. The dazzling sun shone brightly, dousing our cheeks with a touch of red and painting colorful rainbow stripes on the snow-blanketed ridge.

Together we raced our sleds, whizzing down the slick patches of snow. After gliding down numerous times, we were happy to take our nearly frozen bodies home to some welcoming hot chocolate.

People always enjoyed coming to our house on Friday nights. After I became religious, there was an *oneg Shabbos* held regularly at our house. In the winter, our guests would warm themselves, both physically and spiritually, in our home. A warm cup of tea, pretzels, potato chips, and bakery kuchen put everyone in the right spirit. In the summer (in pre–air conditioner days) we gathered next to the fan and relaxed with tall glasses of homemade iced lemonade. Friends and acquaintances would drop by to chat, sing, or just enjoy the Shabbos atmosphere, all year round.

My parents excelled at the mitzvah of *hachnasas orchim* even before they were fully Torah observant. Everyone loved to talk and listen to my amiable father. He had that special quality of making one feel so comfortable. As a matter of fact, they felt so comfortable that it was hard to get anyone to leave. We sometimes tried yawning, glancing at our watches, and giving all sorts of hints, but to no avail. My mother, my father, my brother, and I would occasionally go to sleep and leave our guests debating into the wee hours of the morning.

Passing through the storm door of the little red-brick, shingle-roofed house, I stopped to look around at the familiar surroundings. A soft, royal blue wall-to-wall carpeting had replaced the former green one; the chair in which my mother had read stories to me when I was a little girl looked as fluffy and welcoming as ever, though it was a bit tattered by age.

Mom was already tying on her apron. I suppressed a yawn. "I think we'll go up to bed now. It's been a very long day."

Nodding, she exclaimed, "You go right ahead. The beds are ready."

The emotionally painful ordeal Mom was going through caused her incessant fatigue. Loneliness almost bordering on despair was her daily portion. In the past, she'd have been beaming cheerfully, but now it was different. She had to search for a ride to see my father daily, yet she kept a cheerful countenance in my father's presence. Her faith in the Ribbono shel Olam kept her going. Maintaining the courage to accept each day and continue along the path of sanity was her unspoken motto. It was uplifting when the family members from Israel arrived.

While Laibel deposited our suitcases on the couch, I headed up the stairs to my old bedroom. My daughter and soundly sleeping grandson followed me. The beds were invitingly arranged with crisp matching sheets. Soon ensconced among the feather pillows, we were blessed with peaceful slumber.

The following morning, after davening and eating a light breakfast, I trotted back upstairs to get ready to leave for the hospital. I went into Laibel's former bedroom and opened the cedar closet, breathing in its invigorating scent as I looked over the clothing that had lain untouched for thirty years or more. To my delight, I discovered booties, sweaters, afghans, and other woolen items that my grandmother (may she rest in peace) had knitted or crocheted for my brother and I — all in perfect condition. I chose a few to save for posterity.

Amongst my personal belongings, I came across an old autograph book, dated back to 1962. I found this excerpt on one of the fading yellow pages: "In Cane Park there is a rock, and on it says forget me not. Farther down there is a tree, and on it says remember me." Was it a coincidence? Just yesterday, I'd reminisced about Cane Park and my experiences as a young girl, and now — this autograph book. I think that Hashem wanted to reinforce my childhood past. Experiences teach us many lessons and if we focus on them we can recognize Divine intervention.

Laibel drove us back to the hospital. We secured the baby's hat tightly, turning him into an Antarctic-looking figure. Mom, with her eye on the little "Eskimo" baby, contentedly brought us up-to-date on current events.

Again we made our way through the maze of hospital corridors to my father's room. He was in his glory to have his only great-grandson brought all the way from Israel to him.

"I see you have some visitors again today, Mr. Crystal. That there — your great-grandson, eh?" the nurse smiled with admiration. She was pleased to see my father beaming, his blue eyes shining.

Laibel motioned me aside to attend the meeting with the doctor and better understand the bleak prognosis. "Just take a look at the X rays and you'll see that the stomach area has already been affected...."

The doctor continued speaking, but I was no longer paying close attention. My mind focused my father's fate. If Hashem chose to extend my father's life He would; however, if He felt that the time had come to return his pure soul to Him, I would accept it in full faith. The forecast was dismal. The X rays produced the facts, and nothing short of a miracle could change the situation. Although the doctor predicted that Dad had a maximum of three months to live, I knew that Hashem is the true Source of life. I turned, in silent prayer, to my Creator.

In the elevator, my brother and I discussed Mom's welfare. Thank God, there was a Bikur Cholim organization in Cleveland that arranged car rides for whoever was in need. Mom was often a recipient. Although a young mother had occasionally forgotten her in the supermarket, she generally benefited from the kindness of the volunteers. Still, Mom found it difficult to repeatedly call, taking away her independence.

Returning to the room we photographed the scene. Saba-Rabba (great-grandfather), a wide smile on his face, relished in the *nachas* he received from his great-grandson. We chatted, recalled various events, and enjoyed a memorable experience, providing some happiness for both my parents.

Laibel remarked that before we came, Dad hadn't smiled for

many days. I then understood how a person's illness is partially diminished by visitors. Through this mitzvah of *bikur cholim*, I was able to reunite with my father and bring him extra joy.

Mom had looked weary, with a forlorn look in her hazel eyes, but our arrival changed her mood to a more sunny one.

Though we visited every day of our week-long stay, Saba realized that it was our last day prior to departure and he held the baby tightly, announcing emotionally, "I want to see another one." Tears welled up in his eyes, forcing me to walk out of the room. I knew, deep down in my heart, that only through a miracle would he be able to see another great-grandchild. I cried uncontrollably, then washed my face and returned to say good-bye.

"Dad, let's say *lehitraot*, as they do in Hebrew. It doesn't mean 'good-bye,' rather, 'see you again.' " I gave my father a big hug and a peck on the cheek, looking compassionately into his eyes. My daughter did the same as Saba held the baby for one last time before we parted. Tears were glistening in everyone's eyes when we bade farewell.

Riding back to the house, I wondered whether I would see my father again and knew that the decision was solely up to the Ribbono shel Olam. His decisions are just.

We gathered our belongings quickly to get to the airport on time. It had been a very taxing trip. I was grateful to my daughter's understanding husband, who encouraged her to go and spend this sacred time with Saba. In the short time that my son-in-law had come to know my father, he'd found him to be congenial and fun loving. He didn't want to deny his wife the privilege of seeing her grandfather and showing off their son.

Laibel made the necessary arrangements to transfer Dad to

the Montefiore Nursing Home. He, too, had to return home to his wife and children. Dad mentioned, "I only have insurance to cover a three-month stay in the nursing home. How will I cover the expenses when the time is up?"

Laibel had responded, "We'll cross that bridge when we come to it."

Sunday, March 19, 1997

When I heard the click of the receiver, I was jolted into the present. I had finally reached the airline company. My thoughts centered on the current situation. "Tower Air? Yes, I'd like to reserve a ticket...."

CHAPTER 3

Reactions

Sunday evening, March 9, 1997

Laibel, sweating and loosening his tie, cried out, "Dad, do you hear me?" Turning in the direction of the nurses' station in alarming panic, he said, "Nurse! Nurse! Please come! Something is very wrong here! My father needs medical attention immediately!"

The nurse responded grimly, "You know, Laibel, that your father is terminally ill, and it seems that he's gone into a coma or at least a semicoma. I think you should wait and see what Dr. Gelehrter has to say."

Dejected, Laibel began to pace back and forth as he awaited the doctor's arrival, all the while reciting whatever *tehillim* he knew by heart.

Late Monday afternoon, March 10, 1997

The telephone rang in my house. *Ring, ring* — it shrilled as it sundered the temporary silence in the room. With a bit of apprehension, I reached for the cordless. The long-distance connection was poor, so I could hardly make out the words.

Laibel, full of anguish and utterly choked up, said, "Rivkah, Laibel — Laibel speaking. Dad...seems to have gone into a coma...."

It took a few moments to gather my thoughts and try to dispel my depressed feelings, but a thought came to my mind, and I took advantage of it immediately. "Laibel," I said, trying to hide the tension in my shaking voice, "please, put the phone next to Dad's ear! I — I want to talk to him. I once learned in Rabbi Leff's class that just as a dog can hear a whistle that a human being can't, so too, we don't know to what extent a person in a comatose state can hear."

(I attended classes given by Rabbi Zev Leff, *mara d'asra* of Moshav Matityahu and rabbi of a shul in Har Nof, Yerushalayim, on a weekly basis. I thought about him, in particular, because he had been in the Telshe Yeshiva in our hometown of Cleveland, Ohio, and my father had had a connection with him for many years.)

A bit reluctantly, Laibel put the receiver next to my father's ear. Although the tears welled up in my eyes, I was determined not to let them be detected in my voice. "Daddy, it's me, Rivkah, your doll face. I just want you to know how much I love you. Please wait for me!" I exerted every effort to sound calm.

In a minute, I heard Laibel respond, with excitement in his voice. "Rivkah, I'm sure that he heard you; he squeezed my hand."

I hung up and the tears started to flow, unchecked, from my eyes. An overwhelming feeling engulfed me. Would Hashem allow me to have one more chance to fulfill the mitzvah of *kibbud av va'eim*? Would I be able to make all the arrangements for the children? *Don't panic,* I kept telling myself. *Rivkah, you must take control of the situation! Now is the time for action.*

I thought about *yetzias Mitzrayim,* when the Jewish people

were at the edge of the Red Sea. Some of the people prayed, some wanted to give up and return to Egypt, and a minority was ready to act, either by starting a war or by stepping forth into the sea. Nachshon ben Aminadav, followed by the rest of the nation, treaded into the sea. The waters reached their nostrils, and HaKadosh Baruch Hu parted the sea. They acted and Hashem responded. I realized it was time for me to act, with faith that Hashem would do what was necessary. Perhaps I would now have my own personal miracle, but I was ready to accept whatever the outcome, knowing that the Ribbono shel Olam runs the world.

A few hours later, the phone rang again.

"Hello, Rivkah?" I heard a sigh escape my brother's lips. "Dad's status is unchanged. I'm not so sure anymore — if you should take your trip from Israel to see him." His voice revealed the tension gripping his body and soul. How could Laibel bear it any longer? How could he eat, sleep, or daven like a mensch?

I searched the depths of my mind to formulate a proper response. "Laibel, I really don't know what to do. I'll call Rabbi Leff and see what he has to say. I mean — we already took care of buying a plot here in Beit Shemesh, and what if — what if it should happen, *chas veshalom*, while I'm on the way in, that he'll be flying — out?

"I'm so confused. I'm just not sure what my plan of action should be. Can you please put the phone next to Dad's ear again?" I gathered up my energy in order to sound hopeful for my father.

Placing the receiver next to our father's ear with trepidation, Laibel awaited a response.

"Daddy, hi. It's me, Rivky, calling from Israel. It's your doll face. I love you very much! And I want you to wait for me!"

Laibel said, "Rivkah, I'm sure Dad heard you because he raised his eyebrows!"

Again I felt a sense of relief; a heavy load had just been lifted off of me. I had communicated with my father once more.

The doctors had been in and out of the room the entire day. In my father's hearing range, Dr. Gelehrter told my brother, "Laibel, I'm sorry to have to tell you this, but your father's blood pressure is dropping; his vital organs seem to be in distress and are shutting down."

Taking a deep breath, Laibel responded, "It doesn't look too good, doctor, does it?"

"No, it certainly doesn't. It looks like he has only a few more hours left."

Searching for a ray of hope, Laibel added in entreaty, "But, maybe...?" His words were lost on deaf ears.

Laibel was urged to call the rabbi, as my father's demise seemed imminent.

Only two weeks before, at the end of February, Rabbi Schur had contacted Laibel, urging him to fly in at once, because Dad's strength had waned drastically.

Rabbi Schur was the *rav* of the Heights Jewish Center Synagogue (where my father was a member) and also the kashrus *mashgiach* in the Montefiore Nursing Home. His frequent visits to my father kept him alert to any radical changes in my father. As soon as he became aware of the decline in Dad's medical condition, he phoned Laibel without hesitation.

Laibel grabbed a few meager belongings and was on the first

flight out of Denver. My father perked up tremendously and experienced a new surge of energy. Not more than a day after Laibel's arrival, Dad requested to be escorted home.

"Laibel, please arrange for me to go home. I'd also like to go to the bank and settle a few things."

Laibel was astonished. "Dad, are you sure you're up to this?"

"Of course. I'm feeling much better and I want to go home," Dad responded with resolution. Disregarding his illness and wanting to feel some freedom, my father insisted that he was ready to emerge from his cocoon, even for only a brief time.

With the wheelchair and oxygen tank taken care of, Laibel had to receive an official release from the hospital. Before temporarily discharging Dad, the nurse tested to see if he was limber enough to climb stairs. Dad mounted the small five-step staircase as if he was climbing a mountain.

As comfortable as possible in the passenger seat beside Laibel, Dad looked out the window, absorbing the surroundings. Arriving at the bank gave him a sense of pride. He wanted to take care of his own monetary affairs and walked in proudly, holding his head high. Laibel followed closely, holding the oxygen tank and equipment.

"Mr. Crystal, we haven't seen your cheerful face for quite some time now. It's good to see you." The teller, wearing a broad smile, was happily surprised.

With a carefree attitude, he responded, "I'm happy to be here."

The teller promptly took care of my father, completing all of his monetary transactions.

Then they went home. Mom was quite surprised, even though she'd been notified earlier. Dad sat down in his overstuffed grayish-blue armchair and accepted the hot drink that

Mom had brought him. The room offered a cozy atmosphere.

He then slowly climbed the stairs, using every resource in his spent body, to have a look around at the second story. Everything was just as he remembered it, all furniture, books, and loose odds and ends in their places. The mint-green walls, pink bathroom, and slanted ceilings of the bedroom hadn't changed. Satisfied, he descended and asked if he could stay any longer.

"Dad, your oxygen is running low. We'll have to return to the hospital now," Laibel said kindly.

"Okay, let's go," he sighed, in an unprecedented surrender.

They rode in silence on the return trip, each man immersed in his own thoughts.

Laibel returned to his Denver residence and, just as he was getting back into his regular routine, he had to hastily prepare for another trip to Cleveland. This time he decided to take his wife, Sorah, and their baby.

Laibel's request for a week's leave for personal reasons was granted. The children were "farmed out" to various friends and neighbors. Sorah, the baby, and Mom commuted frequently to the nursing home where Dad was in a special unit, receiving preferential care. They stayed in my parents' home, while Laibel slept on a fairly uncomfortable chair near our father's bed.

On March 11, 1997, a mild Tuesday morning, I once again dialed the number of the Montefiore Nursing Home. It was already 6:30 A.M. in Yerushalayim, but it was only 11:30 P.M. in Cleveland. The seven-hour time difference gave me some time to catch a few hours of restless sleep.

I hadn't yet called Rabbi Leff to ask his advice on flying to Cleveland on Thursday as planned. Still, I felt the need to call and speak to Dad. *Wait for me* were the words constantly on my mind.

Yeshaya asked, "Rivkah, why do you keep telling your dad to wait for you? Maybe it will discourage him."

"I really think that this is precisely what keeps him going. It gives him the hope to carry on."

Hope kept the fire burning in his *neshamah*, which seemed to be attached to his body by a thin thread. I remembered the last Friday night, when I *benched licht*. I watched the flames flickering, thinking of my father. How long would his flickering flame continue to burn? Only the Creator of the Universe held the key to the answer.

The telephone connection between Jerusalem and Cleveland was completed. "Rivkah? No, unfortunately, Dad's condition hasn't changed. He's in a sitting position on the bed, propped up by pillows to help him breath. He hasn't responded to anything, other than a small jerk of his head or clenched teeth when the nurse comes to clean his mouth to keep his breathing passages clear." Laibel's weariness was evident in his faltering voice.

"Laibel, I'd like to try to talk to Dad again; please put the receiver next to his ear."

"He seems so much weaker, but I'll give it a try."

"Daddy dear..." It was rather difficult to keep the calmness in my tone of voice, but *I must,* I told myself. It could be a case of *pikuach nefesh* (saving one's life). "It's Rivkah, your doll face. I love you so much. Daddy, please wait for me! I'm coming, God willing!" I felt that these words had become a signal between my father and myself.

Laibel's voice perked up. "Rivkah, I'm sure he heard you; he squeezed his eyebrows together in a marked sign of recognition. You bring him to life with your soothing words."

Laibel's words reminded me of Yaakov Avinu's granddaughter, Serach, daughter of Asher, when she sang to her grandfather, gently telling him that Yosef was still alive. It had helped to prepare Yaakov for the meeting with his son Yosef, whom he hadn't seen for twenty-two years. Although Yaakov thought that Yosef was dead, his longing for his son never ceased and he harbored the hope that perhaps his son was still alive.

Serach probably prevented Yaakov from experiencing a heart attack. Hearing the shocking news about Yosef still being alive (after so many years of separation) could have resulted in a catastrophe. She was later granted entrance to Gan Eden alive for this mitzvah. She had communicated with her grandfather in a very unique and special way. I now felt relief; once again I had communicated with my dear father in a special, endearing way.

During my morning davening, I beseeched Hashem to intervene on behalf of my dear father, Shlomo Meir ben Sorah Faiga. I was sure that he wanted to see me as much as I wanted to see him.

Later, I phoned my married children and reminded them of the present crisis. They assured me in turn that their *Tehillim* books would be opened and utilized as much as possible during the day.

CHAPTER 4

Mitzvah of the Moment

Slam! Bang! One by one, the children were returning home. Once everyone arrived, it was time to get down to business. I distributed books of *Tehillim* to everyone and explained, "Saba's illness has worsened; it's our duty to say *Tehillim*." In unison, they nodded their heads in the affirmative.

"Children, listen carefully. *Tehillim* are being said all over the world; our prayers will undoubtedly reach Shamayim. Your cousins overseas are also davening for Saba. From Denver to Cleveland to Yerushalayim, HaKadosh Baruch Hu is being beseeched with our heartfelt prayers.

"Please take your *Tehillim* books now and ask Hashem to send a *refuah sheleimah* to Shlomo Meir ben Sorah Faiga."

The children were unusually quiet, listening attentively to my carefully chosen words. We opened our *Tehillim* books and began to pray. Being surrounded by my sweet children helped to ease the strain on my tired body and alleviate some of the emotional stress.

My eight-year-old Moishy had tears streaming down his cheeks as he poured his heart out to Hashem. His twin brother, Saphy (short for Elyasaph), was engrossed in his *Sefer Tehillim*. He, too, had wet eyes.

My ten-year-old Miryam enunciated every word of the *Tehillim*, so that her younger sisters, who couldn't read yet, would be able to repeat after her. *"Hashem hoshea haMelech ya'aneinu b'yom koreinu* — God, who saves, the King who will answer on the day of our calling...."

Rachayli, just past her fifth birthday, sat alongside me faithfully repeating every word that Miryam said, while Chani, all of three years old, sat innocently on my lap, unaware of the magnitude of the present situation. Her smooth, gentle hand was tucked into mine, supplying me with a secure feeling.

Fifteen-year-old Sari arrived last, tiptoeing into the apartment and seating herself beside us. Her brown eyes covered over with a wet mist as she thought about Saba. Silently moving her lips, she swayed back and forth as she recited *Tehillim*.

It was only my personal family. No friends, no homework, and no chores presented interference. Total mindfulness was placed on the mitzvah of the moment.

I recharged my emotional motor and offered my thanks to the Ribbono shel Olam for His assistance.

Laibel's children, each in a different place, poured their hearts out to Hashem, requesting His genuine mercy.

"Eileh varechev ve'eilah basusim va'anachnu b'shem Hashem nazkir — The nations of the world put their trust in chariots and horses [or modern-day tanks and other sophisticated equipment] and we [the Jewish nation] put our trust in God" (*Tehillim* 20:8).

After tucking the children in that evening, I closed my eyes to rest, but instead of falling asleep, my thoughts carried me back to three years ago, when my father's illness first became serious.

CHAPTER 5

Trip to the Kosel

It was back in March of 1994. I remember the day of the operation. My children were gathered together. "Dress warmly, everyone. I know it's freezing cold and windy, but we must go to the Kosel. Saba is having a very serious operation today, and we need to daven for him."

Moishy inclined his head in my direction. "Ima, it's a mitzvah to go, and maybe we can really help Saba. I'm ready. Let's go!"

The rest nodded in agreement and grabbed their coats and hats, and out the door we went.

My husband had been away for two days. The car was not exactly reliable, nor was parking near the Kosel easily accessible. Since we were six people, we were too many to fit into a taxi, so we headed to the bus.

When the old red and white bus arrived, we eagerly climbed on, thankful that it wasn't crowded. We sat huddled together until we came nearer to the Kosel. When some elderly women ascended onto the bus, my five-year-old twin sons jumped up immediately to offer their seats. My sense of pride soared.

"*Tachanah ha'achronah* (last stop)!" cried the bus driver.

We'd arrived safely at the Kosel. Carrying my sleeping Chani in my arms, I held onto two-year-old Rachayli's hand. The other children walked silently by my side, absorbing the peaceful surroundings. The famous Western Wall is where millions of our Jewish brethren have been gathering over the centuries with their prayer supplications.

One stands in awe, approaching the plaza area before descending to the Wall itself. Just to look at the Kosel can send shivers down a Jewish spine. Even the non-Jews stand with reverence before the Kosel — it's awesome. It is a vestige of the past connected to the present, binding them close together.

My husband has taken numerous tourists to visit the Kosel Tunnels and South Wall excavations, where he connects the days of yore to contemporary times. Standing on the street that was once traversed by thousands of Jewish people on their way to offer their sacrifices is captivating.

The Western Wall around the Temple Mount is completely intact. It measures about five American football fields long. When walking through the Kosel Tunnels today, one can observe the Wall in its entirety.

Why is this entire wall (which up until a few years ago was not even thought to exist, other than the small segment known as the Kosel) still in existence? This question can be answered in a few ways.

During the three years that it took to build the Holy Temple it didn't rain during the day, only at night. Hashem was pleased with the building of the Temple and orchestrated the weather in cooperation.

The bulk of the Jewish people used hired laborers to construct the walls of the Beis HaMikdash; however, the poor men, who wanted to help with the building, had no means to employ assistants. Arduous work occupied most of the hours of their days; therefore, the only free moments available to donate to the Beis HaMikdash were from sunrise. Arising early, they erected the Western Wall with their own hands. Although it took blood, sweat, and tears to accomplish this tedious task, the poor men labored on, until it was complete. This was very precious in the eyes of the Ribbono shel Olam. He stipulated that this wall would remain intact forever.

There is one huge stone in the Kosel that has been estimated to weigh four hundred tons. Various theories explain how stones this size were put into the foundation. According to one theory, pulleys were utilized to lift the rocks; another defines techniques involving wheels for rolling the stones. But the theory most congruous with HaKadosh Baruch Hu's pleasure is described in the following *Midrash Tanchuma.*

Rabbi Chanina ben Dosa wanted to bring a gift to contribute to the building of the Beis HaMikdash. He was a righteous yet poor man who possessed neither gold nor silver for his contribution. For days he worked, chiseling a large stone until he felt it was ready to bring to Yerushalayim. Rabbi Chanina ben Dosa now had to find workers to transport the huge stone to Yerushalayim, which was particularly difficult because of his limited means. At last he found suitable workers.

Upon reaching their destination in a relatively short time, Rebbi Chanina ben Dosa lowered his head to seek out the few coins in his possession he'd prepared to pay his workers. When he raised his eyes again, they were gone.

The Sages of the Sanhedrin told him that no man could ever have lifted the massive boulder he'd brought with him; therefore, they had to have been angels of glory sent by HaKadosh Baruch Hu to do the work.

Ever since the Jewish exile, various nations have constantly built on top of, and adjacent to, this Wall. Most of the nations of the world didn't care that it was a holy site to the Jewish people. Eventually, everyone thought the Wall was destroyed, with only the Kosel as the sole remnant. The recent discovery of the entire Wall's remains has demonstrated the truth of Hashem's promise that the Western Wall would remain intact forever.

"Ima, we'll meet you here in about ten minutes. Moishy and I are going to daven in the men's section," exclaimed Saphy.

"Okay, honey. Please remember how important the *tefillos* of *tinokos shel beis rabban* are."

The boys scurried over to the men's section and I took a seat on the women's side of the *mechitzah* close to the Kosel. Shivers traveled down my spine, due to both my emotions and the chill in the air. The *kedushah* of the place in which I stood, ready to offer my prayers, was palpable.

My gaze fell upon the ancient stones, and I could almost hear them whisper, "Pray, pour out your heart and your *tefillos* will go straight up to the heavens. Don't be afraid. Hashem hears you."

Bits of greenery peeked through some of the crevices of the Wall. Pigeons perched themselves at various points, gazing at the worshipers. It was awesome to look up and see how tall the Wall really was. I felt small in comparison. Though I'd been there numerous times, the feeling of awe never diminishes.

Huddling next to the girls to keep them warm, I glowed with the knowledge and comfort that Hashem's Divine presence dwelled there. I closed my eyes and opened my tear-stained *Tehillim* to recite the verses out loud. My girls echoed my every utterance.

The cold air seemed to cut right through us, but we ignored it. When we were finished, we pressed our lips against the Kosel to say *"lehitraot."* We then walked backwards in reverence, re-treating from the Kosel.

In the plaza area, I spotted the twins waiting patiently. We hurried to catch the bus for our journey home. Darkness had already descended upon the city of Jerusalem, but the ray of hope continued to give light.

The very next day I called Dad. "Mr. Crystal, please. This is his daughter calling from Israel."

"One moment, please," was the disembodied response from the secretary. She transferred the call.

"Nn-yello," he said, in a slightly drugged voice. This serious operation rendered him a recipient of pain-relieving drugs.

"Daddy, it's Rivky. How are you feeling?" I inquired.

"Doll face! To tell you the truth, I feel like I've been hit by a Mack truck!" responded my father, in his typical Cleveland accent.

"Dad, I wish you a quick recuperation — a *refuah sheleimah.* I want you to know that yesterday I took the children to the..."

"...to the Kotel," he interrupted me, finishing my sentence.

"How did you know?" I asked in surprise.

"I dreamt that you took the children to the Kotel to daven for me."

"You dreamt it? Really?"

"I did, and I honestly appreciate your effort in going in spite of the inclement weather. You earned a great mitzvah."

"Thanks, Dad. You know that I would do anything for you. We were very happy to honor you."

I marveled at the fact that my father actually dreamt about our journey to the Kosel. He must have felt grateful to the Master of the Universe, his grandchildren, and myself. I felt gratified in the accomplishment and took pride in the children's superb behavior.

Recovery took time. He grew stronger day by day. On Friday, when he was well enough to partake of his first liquids after the operation, he chose to wait for Kiddush. It was his personal way of showing appreciation to the Ribbono shel Olam.

CHAPTER 6

Hodu LaShem

L ate Tuesday afternoon, March 11, 1997, Laibel dosed on and off. Every now and then he glanced in Dad's direction. Detecting some movement, Laibel rubbed his eyes and moved a little closer to Dad. Suddenly Dad vomited, grabbed hold of Laibel's suit jacket, and hollered, "Laibel, sit me up!"

Laibel, white as a sheet, nearly fainted. He caught himself just in time by grabbing the chair.

The nurse on duty heard the commotion and came running in, her hat askew. "Laibel, are you all right? What's going on here?" She paused, then caught sight of Dad. "Mr. Crystal! Well, I'll be! You've got your beautiful blue eyes open. How are you feeling?"

Laibel, after surviving his brush with "*techiyas hameisim*," regained control of the situation and helped my father into the chair. Anxious to hear what Dad had to say, he probed, "Dad, did you hear what was going on?"

Dad, still weak from his coma, whispered, "Yes, Laibel, I heard everything."

Laibel's eyes rolled upwards, as he shook his head, recalling the conversation that had taken place among the doctors early that morning. "Did you hear Rivkah talking to you on the phone?"

"Yes, every time she called, I heard her telling me how much she loves me, and to wait for her." Dad was still very pale. "I want to see her," he added hopefully.

Laibel, concerned about Dad's strength, said, "Dad, I think you should rest for a while. We'll continue this conversation a little later."

Dad dosed off in the chair, breathing heavily but regularly.

Laibel took some deep breaths and a cold drink of water, splashing some on his face. He proceeded to call his wife and Mom to let them know what happened. Everyone responded with shock, thanking the Ribbono shel Olam for His abundant *chesed*.

"I had a feeling that Dad would survive the coma and continue to be a fighter, as he has been many times in the past," Mom said. "*Hodu laShem ki tov, ki le'olam chasdo* — Thank God for His goodness, His kindness prevails forever."

Laibel glanced at his watch to see if it was too late to call Israel. Thinking aloud, he said, "It must be after midnight in Israel and Rivkah must be worn out. I'll wait until morning. She's going to need a lot of energy if she's planning to fly in."

❊   ❊   ❊

At 7:00 A.M., March 12, 1997, very early on Wednesday morning, the phone's ringing upset the quiet atmosphere in our home.

I stopped what I was doing to grab the phone. "Hello, Jacobs residence."

"Rivkah, it's Laibel. I have some good news for you. Are you sitting down?"

"No, Laibel, I don't usually have time to sit down at this early hour of the morning. How's Dad?"

"My dear sister, I think you should sit down," Laibel countered adamantly.

Sitting down, I responded uneasily, "What is it, Laibel? What's happening?"

"Rivkah, this afternoon Dad pulled himself up and spoke to me!"

I could hardly believe my ears. "Laibel, are you serious? Do you mean that Dad's out of the coma?"

"Yes, that's exactly what I mean! I witnessed a miracle! It was *techiyas hameisim* — for me as well as Dad."

"Baruch Hashem," I responded, slowly letting out my breath. I was certain that our *tefillos* on the previous day had been accepted. The tears had pierced the gates of Heaven.

"It was an unbelievable experience. He vomited, pulled himself up, and told me to put him in the chair. I asked him if he'd heard what had been said while he was 'out' and he responded, 'Every word!' " Laibel sounded out of breath.

"It is truly a miracle! Tell me, what does Dr. Gelehrter have to say about all this?" I asked cautiously.

"The doctor? He doesn't know anything about it yet. It all happened just a few hours ago. Only the nurses on duty know. They were dumbfounded. I'll have to wait until tomorrow morning to speak to the doctor. Don't forget, it's only Tuesday night in Cleveland."

"What was Mom's reaction?" I asked.

"Mom said she had a feeling that Dad would pull out of it. She was — rather expecting it."

"When will the doctor be in?" I queried, still absorbing Laibel's news.

"He generally comes in at around 10:00 in the morning. I think I'll try to grab a little sleep. It's been an overwhelming experience and I need to regain my stamina. I'll speak to you tomorrow."

Thoughts churned turbulently in my head, but I didn't

have time to think because I needed to get the children off to school or they'd all be late. When a family is going through a crisis, whether minor or monumental, one of the worst things to do is to change the family schedule. I didn't want any unnecessary interruptions for the children. First and foremost was my role as a mother. This has been my favorite job and I wouldn't trade it for anything. Striving to be a true *eishes chayil* has been the goal of every wife and mother in an observant Jewish home throughout history, and my work and all other responsibilities were secondary.

How we deal with a crisis has a direct influence on how our own children will react in the future to similar situations. I had to try to keep things running as smoothly as possible.

When the door closed behind the children, I once again resumed my deliberations. Should I try to make the trip to Cleveland? Would I get there in time? Finally, I called Rav Leff for his opinion.

"I think that you should base your decision on what the doctor has to say," was the *rav's* wise answer.

❊   ❊   ❊

A few hours later, I was dialing the doctor. In the three-minute waiting period from the time the secretary paged Dr. Gelehrter, I felt my heart palpitating. Static sounds emanated from the transatlantic line to Cleveland, Ohio. I wondered how to phrase my urgent question.

"Dr. Gelehrter, this is Rivkah Jacobs, Mr. Crystal's daughter, calling from Israel. I'd like to ask your professional medical opinion." I paused to regain composure. "Do you think I would be able to see my father if I flew in?" It was hard to keep my voice steady enough to get all the words out clearly.

Dr. Gelehrter hesitated. "Listen, Mrs. Jacobs, I didn't expect to see your father here today at all! I don't know what to say. All I can say is, if you're a gambler, then take the risk and come."

The first piece of the puzzle was put into place.

Gambling was in my blood. It could have fortified my veins. Before my father had become religious, he'd gambled with cards or bet on horses, but those were days belonging to yesteryear. (Later in his life he gambled only for charitable causes.)

Whenever I had an urge to gamble, I utilized this character trait for a positive cause. I would take our *ma'aser* money and head out to Chinese auctions and gamble away, knowing that the money would be used to help a yeshivah or impoverished brides. Here, again, I was being asked to gamble — take the risk and perform a mitzvah. Travel to America and see my father.

The various characteristics we are born with can be used negatively or positively. For example, a person who is endowed with a murderous tendency can either become a killer — a threat and burden to society — or a *shochet*, who performs the mitzvah of slaughtering kosher animals in accordance with Jewish law (which also causes less suffering for the animals) and is an asset to the Jewish people.

My turn had come. How would I employ my inborn qualities? I had to be steadfast in my resolve. I fell asleep that night under mounting stress. In the morning I'd have to make my final decision.

CHAPTER 7

Decisions

Thursday morning, March 13, 1997

It was 7:00, time to get the children ready for school.

"Rivkah?" Yeshaya called my name questioningly.

"Yeshaya?" I replied.

"I've made a decision. You're going!" my husband said emphatically.

Still half asleep, I said, "Going where?"

"You're going to see your father! I have a feeling you'll make it. Get on the phone and book your ticket."

Obediently I answered, "Okay! First let's get the kids ready for school on time. The offices don't open until nine o'clock anyway, and right now it's 7:04. And besides, don't you remember that I booked a ticket at the beginning of the week? It's just a matter of picking it up."

My head was swimming. Shaya had made a decision that I was going to stick with; I had just been too apprehensive to follow through without his approval. I could see that in Hashem's big puzzle, the pieces were starting to fall into place.

"I'd better take a pen and paper and jot down today's itinerary so that I don't forget anything important."

I started a priority list:

1. Do a load of laundry and straighten up the house.

2. Tape all lists to appropriate places (washing machine instructions on its door, chores and menus on the fridge, etc.).

3. Call airline office to pick up international ticket.

4. Call Sussy Abramowitz (the travel agent) for ticket to Cleveland.

Getting the children ready for school was imperative. "Miryam, can't you find your other white sock?" I snapped. "I guess you'll just have to wear the blue ones whether you like it or not!"

I could hear Miryam whispering to the other children, "Watch out! Ima's on the warpath."

An hour later, the little girls were dressed and ready. Yeshaya would drop them off at school. On his way out the door, he said, "After I drop off the girls, I'll be going into town to take care of a few things. I'll be in touch with you a little later."

"I'll try to work on the tickets as soon as I finish davening. Thanks, Shaya, and have a good morning."

As I grabbed the girls' lunches and stuffed them into their schoolbags, I felt my nerves frazzling. "Quick, Abba's waiting for you in the car. Go!" It was almost a "good riddance" bellow.

The *yetzer hara* has a way to find himself in our homes precisely when he's least wanted. I knew that my actions and reactions were not consistent with what I preach, but we all have the human element involved, causing us to occasionally fall short. I'm thankful that Torah Judaism allows us to pick ourselves up and rise again. I'd apologize to my children when they came home, as my actions were uncalled for.

The moment I noticed that Yeshaya had forgotten the cell phone, I dashed to the window, gesticulating and waving my arms, but to no avail. The phone remained abandoned on the table.

I took my siddur and tried to concentrate on the words of the prayers, but I found my mind wandering. I tried again and again, but I just couldn't concentrate. Picking up speed, I said the words quickly in order to get on with the mitzvah I needed to accomplish. Would it become mission impossible?

Finishing my rushed prayers, I asked Hashem to help everything work out. If I was meant to make this trip to see my father, obtaining a ticket should go smoothly and further obstacles should be removed from my path.

I speedily threw a load into the washing machine and dashed around putting all the prepared lists into place. The time went fast. It was soon 11:00, and I'd hardly managed to get anything done.

Now on to the nitty-gritty. "Tower Air? I'd like to come down to pay for my reserved ticket. It's under the name of Mrs. Rivkah Jacobs."

I waited anxiously while the secretary fiddled around with the computer. *Maybe her computer is slow today*, I thought.

"I'm sorry, but you should have picked up that ticket two days ago; you no longer have a reservation," she said at last.

CHAPTER 8

The Tickets

"What? Will you please repeat that?" I was dumbfounded.

"Yes, *geveret*, tickets not redeemed within the time limit are forfeited," she said coolly.

I didn't know what to say next but relied heavily on *siyatta diShmaya*. "So I'll purchase another ticket. Is there another seat available on that flight?" I inquired pleadingly.

"No, I'm really sorry, there are no more seats available." She answered more softly this time, probably detecting panic in my voice.

"Are you sure there are no vacant seats on the flight? My father is extremely ill and I must get onto this flight."

"Listen, I'm really sorry. I wish I could help you, but I can't manufacture another seat on this flight."

I was not going to give up so easily. "Do you mean to tell me that there are no seats left on the entire plane? Please look it up in your computer again — maybe you'll find a seat in any section!"

Silence. I could hear the second hand on my wristwatch ticking away almost as loud as my heartbeat. I waited, drumming my fingers against the tabletop, for what seemed to be an eternity.

Finally, the agent announced, "Okay, I found you a seat in the business economy class, but it's a more expensive ticket. Do you want it?"

"Of course I want it!"

"You have until 12:00 to pick it up. It's the last seat on the plane, so don't be late."

Looking through my handbag for my wallet, I thought, *I can't believe that Yeshaya didn't take the cellular phone. How am I going to reach him? I have less than an hour to get to the Tower office.*

Rummaging through my pocketbook for cash, I thought, *This is ridiculous. I don't even have enough cash to pay for a taxi!*

"Please, Hashem, don't forsake me now. You've brought me this far, so please help me in my endeavor to accomplish my mission."

Although the cold March wind was blowing, I felt the perspiration forming on my forehead and dripping down my neck and back. Yet I had a gut feeling that Hashem would come to my rescue.

I placed my head on the desk for a second to regain composure. The ringing of the phone startled me, and I jumped up to answer it.

"Rivky, it's me, honey. Is everything all right?" Shaya's voice was most welcome to my ears. How could he possibly know what I'd gone through in the last hour?

It was now 11:30. I blurted out, "Please come and get me quickly. I've got less than a half hour to get to the Tower office. I'll be waiting outside and I'll explain the details later. Just rush!"

Hanging up, I realized that I hadn't phoned Mrs. Abramowitz. With a shaking hand, I reached for the telephone directory. Frantically flipping through the pages, I found her number and dialed.

"Can I help you?" asked Mrs. Abramowitz. I needed her efficient assistance in purchasing a round-trip ticket to Cleveland. She and I had both grown up in its suburbs and she knew my father.

"Sussy, it's Rivkah Jacobs. I need a ticket for a flight from New York to Cleveland for tomorrow morning. It's an emergency! I'm flying out tonight, *b'ezras Hashem*, to see my father who's extremely ill. Please say you have a ticket for me."

Checking her computer, she declared, "Rivkah, I've come up with something. You can have a ticket for $450 round trip from New York to Cleveland."

"I'll take it. I'll be there in about an hour, so please hold the ticket," I answered hurriedly, breaking the connection. The price quote seemed outrageously high for an hour-long local flight, but I wasn't going to argue about it. The main object: a ticket was awaiting me.

Greeting Shaya with a nod of my head in the direction in which we were to proceed, I sat down and tried to relax, leaning back onto the headrest. It wasn't for long.

As we pulled onto Route 1, I could see the traffic jam just ahead of us. Cars were moving at snail's pace. This only added to my tension.

Yeshaya also tensed as the car slowed to five kilometers an hour. Traffic jams were not exactly his favorite cup of tea. In order to ease the tension a bit, I popped a music tape into our tape deck. The young choir had a soothing effect on both of us.

I glanced at the dashboard clock — 11:49 A.M. With only eleven minutes left, and about sixteen minutes of traveling time to go, I realized we weren't going to get there on time. *Baruch Hashem*, although I'd exited hastily, I had remembered to bring the cell phone.

"Tower Air? This is Mrs. Jacobs. I'm supposed to be in your office by 12:00 to pick up my ticket, but we hit an unbelievable traffic jam. Can you wait for about another fifteen minutes? I must fly out tonight to see my father immediately as — as — he is critically ill."

"Okay, but hurry!"

Click. I looked at the cellular phone in my hand and managed a small but meaningful prayer of gratitude to my Maker.

At last we pulled up alongside the Tower Air building. I opened the car door and said to Yeshaya, "Hopefully this won't take too long."

"Fortunately, I brought along my *mishnayos.* I'll try to pull over and wait, but I may have to drive around the block a few times. Go ahead."

My watch read exactly 12:10. I mounted the stairs two at a time, dashing up the two flights to my destination.

Out of breath, I swung the door open and approached the nearest clerk. "Hi, I'm Mrs. Rivkah Jacobs. A round-trip ticket to New York is being held for me in the business economy class."

The woman answered curtly, "Someone will be with you in a minute. Have a seat."

The wait seemed to me endless, but in reality it was only ten minutes (unless my watch had stopped in favor of the clerk). With my ticket tucked firmly inside my pocketbook, I scurried down the two flights, rushing out into the brisk air to look for the van. When my husband pulled up, a questioning look on his face, I got in the car and told him, "*Baruch Hashem*, I have the ticket. Now, let's be off to Sussy Abramowitz for the Cleveland extension of it."

This time we were blessed with *kefitzas haderech* and in almost record time we arrived in the Mattersdorf section of Yerushalayim. Although Yeshaya offered to dash up the three and a half flights for me, I chose to complete this mitzvah on my own.

As I sat next to Sussy Abramowitz's computer, waiting for the results of my ticket, I thought about this electronic, scientific age we live in. Had I been born two hundred years earlier, I would not have been able to make an eleven-hour flight to see a sick loved one. I shuddered to think about my ancestors who may have been in similar situations and about those unfortunate ones who may have been wired a death notice and sat shivah long after their loved ones had passed on to the *Olam HaEmes*.

My thoughts were interrupted when Sussy lifted her gaze from the monitor and announced in amazement that my ticket had come out with a figure much less than the original price quote. "That will be $169 in total."

"How is that possible? Maybe there's a mistake?" I asked incredulously.

"No, the way the ticket comes out of the computer is the price you pay and that's it!" was Sussy's swift response. "Are you sure you still want to take the 6:45 A.M. flight? I can just as easily book you on a flight two and a half hours later, which would still allow you to arrive with time to spare before Shabbos."

"No, I'll keep this flight. Time is of essence in this situation. Thanks for your offer anyway."

I thanked her again as I handed her a check. At this point, I breathed a profound sigh of relief. Walking away I pulled out my pocket calculator. The difference in the sum total of $281 to upgrade to business economy class was the exact amount of money I'd just saved on the ticket to Cleveland. The Almighty doesn't make mistakes. His calculations are exact. Another piece of the puzzle had been put into place.

CHAPTER 9

Ready for Takeoff

Arrival at the home front brought forth lots of anxious children's questions. Letting my husband handle the answers, I rushed to pack for my imminent journey. I wisely decided to take only hand luggage to avoid waiting in the bustling John F. Kennedy Airport. Bare essentials were less than neatly packed into a little blue overnight suitcase, while my passport and tickets were placed into my pocketbook. Just in time, I remembered to arrange the airport taxi service. I then spent the remaining time with my children and husband, giving them the attention they rightfully deserved.

I fixed a quick supper and we sat down to eat. I reminded the children to do their chores, help each other, try to stay on their best behavior, and keep the mitzvah of *ve'ahavta lerei'acha kamocha* as top priority. Whatever mitzvos they fulfilled would only help Saba.

"Children, I want to apologize for the way I behaved this morning. I think I acted a little rude," I said.

Almost in unison, they responded, "It's okay, Ima."

"You were just nervous, it's normal," were Miryam's kind words.

Giving an affectionate kiss and hug to each of my progeny,

I bid them farewell. I felt my throat constrict, but held back the tears. Why spoil our parting by letting the dam erode?

My purpose for this journey was my mitzvah of *kibbud av va'eim*, but I would miss my sweet, dear offspring. My heart skipped a beat when I heard the honk of the airport taxi, beckoning me. Taking the last available seat in the van, I managed to wave good-bye to my family through the window before we were off.

At the airport, to my surprise, I was checked in quickly. Sitting alone at the departure gate, I tried to read a book to settle myself down, but my mind kept drifting off to scenes from the past.

Suddenly, I heard the announcement, "Passengers to New York, please get ready to board the flight."

I was in no hurry to be first to enplane as this would only add to my claustrophobic feeling, so I took my time. Finally I got in line for the bus that would bring the passengers to the plane. I wanted to cry and release my pent-up feelings, but I did not want to attract the attention of my fellow passengers.

When I found my seat on the airplane, I was astonished to see vacant seats on all sides. The airline worker had told me emphatically that I was receiving the last seat on the plane. Here, I witnessed, to my utter amazement, numerous empty seats.

After making myself comfortable, I began a conversation with the lady sitting in the aisle seat. "I was told that there were no available seats left on this flight. If you just look around you, you'll notice that all the middle seats are empty!"

Stifling a yawn, she replied drily, "This is business economy class, and they don't sell the middle seat."

I turned my crimson face to the window to hide my embarrassment. How could I know? I'd never traveled business economy class. In first class you get a wider, more comfortable seat, but leg room was no more ample than it was in regular class.

Soon the jet engines revved up and we began to ascend. I felt physically as well as spiritually close to the Ribbono shel Olam. Looked out into the darkness, I realized my minuteness in comparison to the vastness of all of Hashem's creations. I sensed the *hashgachah peratis* everywhere. An inner voice told me that HaKadosh Baruch Hu would allow my journey to be successful.

I tried to read and listen to some soft music, but nothing calmed my nerves. Closing my eyes brought me back to my childhood and I began to reminisce.

Dad used to play Monopoly with me. Sprawled out on the carpet, we played a great game. Dad was always there for us, whether it was a board game or anything else.

Dad had been the first Jew to be accepted to work for the General Electric Company....

CHAPTER 10

Coping with Anti-Semitism

When relating the story of the light bulb corporation, Dad didn't miss any of the details. "Everyone else had to get 70 percent to pass the test of general acceptance, but I, a Jew born in the United States, had to receive a minimum of 90 percent. They even tried to mix me up with very tricky questions. When I passed, they had no choice but to accept me."

He'd been constantly hassled and occasionally harassed for being Jewish, but he'd always retort with an answer that would catch them off guard. When he started observing the mitzvos, the goyim would talk about the Jewish "beanies." My father rebutted, "Your Pope also wears one!" This answer closed the conversation. Dad usually wore a cap to avoid unpleasant remarks.

When he began to observe Shabbos, he was reminded, in no easy terms, that the other Jews worked on Saturday, so why did he have to be different? (The "other Jews" included other Jewish acquaintances he helped provide with jobs. They were not yet Torah observant.) My father's reply to this one was, "They pray in a different synagogue."

Most of the workers liked and respected him. Whenever they sold candy as a fund-raising endeavor, he always purchased one. (At $1 per chocolate bar, it was quite an extravagant expense at the time.) We often threw them in the garbage because they were not kosher. On occasion he'd bring home a candy bar with the OU kosher symbol on it. We'd get very excited and enjoy our delectable treat.

Among his various work-related experiences, some were funny, others sad, and a few serious.

One morning, Dad bolted out the door after waking up late and arrived at the job just in time to punch the time clock. When he returned home for dinner, his mood was less than amiable. "Dad, what's up?" I prodded.

"This morning I ran out the door with a bag of onions instead of my bagged sandwiches for lunch. I almost choked on liquid soap, instead of drinking soup from my thermos bottle, and you ask, 'What's up?' I'd say I'm hungry as a horse!"

My brother and I, finding this hilarious, muffled our giggles. After supper we could laugh and joke about this incident together. First a meal, or as Mom would always say, "The best way to a man's heart is through his stomach." "Wait until after dinner" was a regular rule in the house.

He was the expert in his unit of the General Electric plant, understanding the mechanics of the light bulb machines. For assistance the workers didn't turn to the foreman, but rather to my father.

Dad could have pursued a career as an engineer, but he came from a family of ten children and feeding them took precedence over my father's higher education. After completing the eleventh grade, he found a job to help support the family. Jack, his older brother, was the main breadwinner of the family.

His father's heart condition made him unable to work on a steady basis. It pained Dad to watch his father pull his cart to peddle rags. They couldn't afford a horse to draw the cart.

Dad told us once, "It hurt me so to see my father with that cart. One day I decided to help him. I took an axe and chopped the cart to pieces. Having his only source of livelihood taken away was too much for my father to bear. Broken in spirit, he refused to speak to me for a full three months."

Solemnly, I interjected, "Dad, how did you feel when he refused to speak to you?"

"It was the worst punishment I ever received in my entire life! My mother used to hit me once in a while, but the pain would subside quickly. Not being able to communicate with my dear father was a severe penalty, especially since my intention had been to help him."

"Didn't he realize that you only meant to spare him from his arduous labor?"

"He had a weak heart and was hospitalized a few times, but he also had his pride. Pulling that cart was his whole life. Selling rags was still some sort of income to support the family. In my short-sightedness, I overlooked his emotional connection to his beloved cart. I was only a young, inexperienced boy, not yet acquainted with life's intricacies. I understand now what I didn't then. His not speaking to me was only natural under his duress."

When my father informed the G.E. Company of his decision to remain home for the Sabbath, they weren't eager to let him off and tried all kinds of means to get him to continue coming in on Shabbos.

One last approach was, "Sam, you won't even have to drive your own car. We'll pick you up and bring you back. You would just have to sit and direct other workers, without doing any work of your own. You'll receive time and a half for your pay."

The extra money was enticing, as factory workers were just managing to make ends meet, but my father was firm in his decision to keep Shabbos. He adamantly rejected their offer.

One day, a big burly gentile named Ray, who was very respectful of Dad, overheard some malicious men discussing my father in the rear room of the factory. They were saying some very anti-Semitic things. He strolled over to the group, flexing the muscles in his arms, and told them in no uncertain terms, "If you guys say one more word about Sam, you'll have to answer to me!"

That was the end of their discussion. Ray proved that there were a few righteous gentiles among the group.

Anti-Semitism intensified among some of the workers when G.E. offered my father the position of foreman. He was one of the few competent workers who could successfully handle the responsibilities of the job, and his coworkers were aware of this fact. The promotion offered would upgrade his status from blue-collar to white-collar worker (which was not only more prestigious, but also provided a higher salary). He strolled out to the parking lot in a happy mood, but to his utter dismay, he found that his car tires had been punctured. A sharp note on the windshield informed him that if he didn't give up the notion of becoming foreman, he could expect more pranks of this sort. This was accompanied by a warning to watch out for his life.

My parents used to refer to the goyim that Dad worked with as "*pruste goyim*" (common gentiles), due to their lack of formal education. They would boast of how many items they were able to steal during their vacations, including televisions, mattresses, and other expensive paraphernalia. He came to the conclusion that their threats were serious and turned down the offer of top foreman, instead becoming the assistant foreman.

Needless to say, he met the ongoing challenges in dealing

with anti-Semitism and was able to set an example of superb behavior both at work and at home.

As I grew older, there were other, more important issues he
had to deal with, especially as my brother and I were becoming
more Torah observant.

CHAPTER 11

Our Relationship

Dad came home from work one day in 1972 very happy. Proudly, he announced to my mother, my brother, and I, "Guess what? I didn't press the soup button today!"

We gaped in astonishment. As my brother and I were constantly working on improving my father's level of *Yiddishkeit*, this was a real milestone.

He continued in a serious tone, "Every day, until today that is, I would press the soup button at work. After all, the children were not there to watch me. Today I turned over a new leaf and decided to take a coffee instead of *treif* soup. I'm sure the children will be proud of me."

Clapping for joy, Laibel and I responded, "Wow, Dad! We really are very proud of you!"

I distinctly recall Dad's devotion to his mother. When she needed him, she'd call, "Shloimela, I need a *toiva*...." He'd be out the door in a flash. Whenever he was in a dangerous situation, he was always spared; I attributed it to his mastering of the mitzvah of *kibbud av va'eim*. He certainly set a beautiful example in our home.

My Bubby, may she rest in peace, was an illustrious woman with a very dominant character. She'd come to family *simchah*s dressed in her gray, short, curly *sheitel*, minimal jewelry, and neat dresses. Like a typical grandmother, she was plump and fun to hug. Her hands and face were wrinkled with age and hard work, a testimony to her difficult life.

Apple strudel was one of her specialties; her only measuring cup was her own hand. Who could follow her delicious recipe if their hand was not the same size as hers?

Her claim to fame was her expertise in cooking, baking, and cleaning, since she had never learned to read or write. Everyone respected her, but only about a quarter of the grandchildren understood her, as she insisted on answering our English with Yiddish. Yiddish was my parents' "secret code" language (spoken occasionally when they did not want my brother and I to understand), but my Yiddish improved by listening to her.

One of my fondest memories of my Bubby is her reaction to my engagement. She asked me in her mother tongue, "*De gaits zan a kosher kallah* — Are you going to be a kosher bride?" (She was referring to my immersion in the *mikveh* prior to my wedding.)

Because I had become Torah observant, it was primarily a rhetorical question. "Of course, Bubby!"

Her eyes lit up with true delight and we hugged each other in an emotional moment. She was so thankful that her granddaughter, daughter of her *ben zekunim*, would be going to a kosher *mikveh*.

When she offered her traditional wedding dress gift, I told her, "I plan on borrowing the dress and using your money to buy a silver *leichter* to *bench licht* with. Bubby, a wedding dress is worn once, but a silver *leichter* will remind me of you every Friday night."

She was convinced, and a new tradition began in our family. When my brother became engaged, she no longer offered a wedding dress, only a sterling silver candelabra.

My marriage to a *talmid* of the Mirrer Yeshiva had a direct connection to my father. How did my father merit having his daughter marry under a proper *chuppah*? Why did so many *roshei yeshivah* dance so fervently at my *chasunah*?

For a bit of extra income, Dad took a part-time job in the Academy Party Center (where I was later married). He tended the bar for various affairs, including bar mitzvahs and weddings. The person responsible for the affair would customarily pay the bartender. Whenever a child of a *rosh yeshivah* would marry, Dad would not only cry throughout the entire *chuppah*, but would also show great respect to the family. When the *rosh yeshivah* would come to pay him, he would say, "It's my present to the *chassan* and *kallah*!"

When my grandfather was alive, we would often visit him and my grandmother together in their Cleveland home. He spoke Yiddish peppered with English, wore a black yarmulke that covered most of his balding head, and sported a mustache that ran straight across his upper lip.

I sat in my grandfather's sukkah as a little girl. I'm convinced that in the merit of his sukkah, my own brother and father were able to perform the mitzvah of building and dwelling in a sukkah years later.

Sukkos 1968

"Laibel, if you insist on having a sukkah, I'm willing to contribute $10," Dad told my brother.

"Listen, Dad, I bought the wood and the nails in order to build a small sukkah. It came out to $11.38."

"Okay, Laibel. I'll pay for the whole thing and you'll have your sukkah."

Sukkos 1996

With all the strength he could muster, my father slowly shuffled the fifteen-minute distance to David Rosenbaum's sukkah so that he could make Kiddush in a kosher sukkah. (His illness prevented him from building his own.) He had no intention of missing this mitzvah. Triumphantly, he recited the blessing over the wine.

In honor of my grandfather's seventy-fifth birthday, my brother and I saved our pennies for months in a small piggy bank. Finally, we hit seventy-five. We brought our special gift (and life savings) to our grandfather. He gave us a broad smile, displaying some gold teeth from the old country. "*A groisse danke schoine.*"

He immediately began distributing the pennies to all the little children who came to honor him on his birthday. At the time, my brother and I were devastated. All those hard-earned pennies squandered so quickly! As time went on and we looked back, we realized his greatness. His pleasure and happiness were to give to others and not leave even a "penny" for himself. My grandfather, in his own way, taught me how to give with one's full heart.

He was ten years older than my Bubby, but she seemed to make the decisions in their family. They'd been married in Russia-Poland when she was a mere fifteen years old. Their first daughter was born when she was sixteen, followed by five more daughters. My grandfather then went to work in America for seven years to bring his family to its shores.

My Bubby, who had been pregnant when he left, gave birth to her very first *yingele* a short time later. She had to take care of all the preparations for the bris by herself. She even had to send a picture to my grandfather, as the story goes, because after having six girls he wanted to be sure that this was really a boy. Yaakov Moshe, affectionately called Yankel (later known as Jack in the United States) didn't get to meet his father until he was seven years old, when my grandfather finally earned enough money to send them tickets for the transport ship.

My father was the third boy to be born to the Crystal family unit. He was the third child to be born in America and was named Shlomo Meir ben Chaim Yehuda at his bris. His English name became Sammy.

I finally dozed off. The plane had been flying steadily, accompanied by the monotonous hum of the engines. Suddenly, the loudspeaker crackled to life, awakening me. "Fasten your seat belts. Put your seats in upright position. We have to make a refueling stop in Scotland. You will be allowed off the plane to stretch your legs, but no one is permitted out of the terminal."

CHAPTER 12

Unforeseen Events

I shook my head, perplexed. Perhaps I was dreaming. I turned to my neighbor and asked, "This is not a scheduled stop, is it?" This was basically a rhetorical question; we both knew the answer.

"No, it certainly is not!" she answered, quite as perturbed as I was.

How much would the refueling delay us? I had to switch airports in New York to catch my next flight. What if I missed it? How would I get to Cleveland on time?

Rivkah, grab a hold of yourself! This entire voyage is happening because Hashem wanted it to occur. If this is Hashem's desire and He wants you to get to Cleveland on time, then you will arrive as planned. Worrying about it will not bring the desired results. Tefillah will. Get out your Tehillim and get busy.

I felt a little calmer after this mental message. Most of the passengers were yawning, fidgeting, and looking quite cranky. Sitting in the Scotland airport, I recited some *tehillim*, but I couldn't help fidgeting, glancing at my watch every few minutes. A total *malach* I can't claim to be.

Before I knew it we were boarding, resuming our journey to New York. The video screen displayed a map showing exactly where we were and how much longer it would take to reach our destination. I knew that we had lost a bit more than an hour, but perhaps the winds would help us gain some time and Hashem would see to it that I make it to my destination punctually.

I fell asleep for close to half an hour and awoke with just an hour left to New York. Would I still be able to catch my flight to Cleveland?

I stopped the stewardess to explain my situation, asking permission to sit in first class among the first passengers to deplane. Kindly, she found me a temporary seat in first class.

Forty minutes left to go. I tried to suppress gloomy thoughts. Barely having slept, I ate the unappetizing airline breakfast and anxiously contemplated the imminent landing. Closing my tired eyes, I dozed for about fifteen minutes (bringing my total sleep record on the flight to approximately one hour and forty minutes).

The "fasten seat belts" sign was on again, and the pilot came on the loudspeaker with the announcement, "Please put your seats in upright position, as we are preparing for landing. We hope you enjoyed your trip. Those of you who will need assistance, please let the nearest flight attendant know."

Within half an hour, the plane descended and my ears began to pop. When we hit the ground, many passengers started applauding. I quickly grabbed my coat, pocketbook, and hand luggage and briskly headed for the exit sign, only to be met with resistance. Stewardesses blocked all exits. A doctor on board was attending to a cardiac arrest patient, who had to be transported to the hospital for emergency medical care. For me it was another test from the One Above, and I knew I had to keep my head on my shoulders, ready to fly the minute we received the all-clear signal. *Baruch Hashem*, it wasn't long in coming.

I cleared customs and scurried as fast as my legs would carry me to the exit. My dear husband's words rang in my ears: "Remember to take a yellow cab and not a regular car service, as you never know who the driver may be. Yellow cabs are registered and safer."

A brisk wind hit my face when I stepped past the heavy glass door to the outside world of New York City. It was still very early in the morning; the yellow cabs were nowhere in sight. They would show up in around an hour, when the rest of the passengers emerged with their baggage.

CHAPTER 13

Time Is of Essence

I always understood that HaKadosh Baruch Hu was with me, but when a car service pulled up within half a minute of the time I walked out of the revolving door, I felt it even more. The car pulled up to the curb and the driver shouted, "Need a taxi, lady?" It just had to be for me! Yellow or not, here I come.

"Yes," I cried. "Please get me to La Guardia Airport fast. My plane leaves in twenty-five minutes!"

"You got it, lady. We're off." As he zoomed down the street, I caught my breath, wondering if I was on the world's largest roller coaster or again on the jet runway.

Driving up the massive highway, we unfortunately hit a traffic jam. I felt my patience running low. "How long will take us to get to the airport?"

My driver, who had a crew cut and a black leather jacket, had probably grown up in Little Italy. Undaunted by the traffic, he calmed me, "Don't worry, lady, you'll make it. Gonna get there in 'leven minutes."

The cabbie knew his business — eleven minutes it was. The bill came to $26. I handed him a twenty and a ten, telling him to keep the change. There was simply no time to wait. With a broad smile he said, "You're gonna make it, lady."

My handbag, pocketbook, and I successfully passed through the metal detector, and I sprinted down the airport hallway at top speed. Panting and totally out of breath, I reached the terminal. I pulled out my ticket for verification of the flight number.

"Ma'am, you just made it! You'd better get onto that plane right this second or you's not gonna make it. Hurry! Wait, ain't you got no luggage?" The airport employee's pearly white teeth shone against her black face.

Catching my breath, I answered, "No — no luggage," and proceeded rapidly down the plank leading to the entrance of the plane.

"Please take your seat, as the plane is ready for takeoff," the stewardess told me.

My legs aching from the marathon, I managed to find my seat. I fastened my seat belt and the plane began to taxi. However, we ended up remaining on the ground of La Guardia Airport for at least half an hour as the plane was deiced.

Fearing the worst, I thought, *Could it be Hashem's desire to have me grounded in the New York airport?* Eventually, however, we were on our way.

Adjusting my ears to the cabin pressure, I dozed off for a short time. When I awoke, beverages and a snack of pretzels were served. It was quite a relief to see the OU on the snack; I was already famished and it helped calm my growling stomach.

The flight was less than an hour, but the takeoff and landing took almost as much time as the actual flight. I'd arranged with my brother that he should pick me up, because I would have no time to call before boarding the plane. Fortunately, he called the airline to find out the arrival time and was informed of the delay.

After deplaning, I bounded for the airport exit. The second

the bitter-cold Cleveland air struck my exposed face, my brother pulled up in my father's car. I was, once again, grateful to the Ribbono shel Olam.

"*Baruch Hashem*, you made it. I wish this meeting was for a joyous occasion." Laibel had a distraught look on his normally cheerful face.

"Laibel, it was a harrowing journey; you can't imagine all the stumbling blocks along the way. Beyond the shadow of a doubt, I sensed Hashem's presence every step," I assured him.

Silence prevailed as we drove until Laibel said, "I'm taking you directly to see Dad. I don't have to tell you how critical his situation is."

"How much longer is the ride?"

"It'll be about another fifteen minutes, if we don't hit any morning rush-hour traffic."

We then discussed the approaching Shabbos. Yeshaya had said that Laibel should have a break and stay at home with my sister-in-law, their baby, their sixteen-year-old son, Avraham (who was learning in Telshe Yeshiva), and my mother. I should be the one to spend Shabbos with Dad. Laibel agreed with Yeshaya's proposal, and it was settled before we arrived at the Montefiore Home.

I could feel butterflies fluttering in my stomach. Soon I would finally be with my dear father. How would he look? Would he recognize me or know that I was with him? My feet propelled me through the hallways in the direction of his room.

Approaching the nurses' station, I saw the head nurse on the phone. She looked up at me and said, "Are you Rivkah Jacobs?" When I replied in the affirmative, she handed me the phone. "It's for you. It's your husband."

I could see the pieces of the puzzle falling into place from every angle: the car service, the flight, my brother's arrival at the split second I walked out of the airport, and my husband's international call at precisely the time of my arrival. I took the receiver from her outstretched hand.

"Rivky, how's your father?" came Shaya's question. "How was your flight?"

"I haven't even seen Dad yet. I just got here this minute, and the nurse handed me the phone. I'm very anxious to see Dad; I'll fill you on all the details later. If I don't speak to you again before Shabbos, give hugs, kisses, and my love to all the children. Remind them to daven for Saba."

"Okay. Remember, we're all thinking about you and praying for Dad."

Removing my coat, I took a deep breath before entering the room. My father was propped up in bed, eyes closed, breathing evenly. He looked a bit on the sallow side, but not unusual. Slowly I moved to his side and bent down beside him. "Daddy, it's me, Rivky. I'm here. I came all the way from Israel to see you. I'm going to spend Shabbos with you."

Dad squeezed his eyebrows together, tightening his facial muscles in the way that Laibel had described last time when he was in a semicoma. I knew that we had communicated; Hashem had answered my prayers. Although I realized that his strength was waning, the special sign he'd just given was very precious to me.

I called Laibel over to report the facts. Then I turned to my father again. "Daddy, please wait for me. I'm going to the house to pack what I need for Shabbos, but I'll be back shortly. Wait for me! You've waited this long; just wait a little longer so that we can spend Shabbos together." On that note, I squeezed his hand and left the room, Laibel at my side.

As we pulled into the driveway, Mom rushed to the door to see me. I ran to give her a hug and a kiss.

"Mom, you can't imagine how happy I am to have arrived safely."

I had a few hours to shower and get dressed for Shabbos. Mom prepared a package of food for me to take with me. (My father had been provided with kosher food at the home, but at the moment, he was being fed intravenously.)

Mom was putting the last touches on her Shabbos meal preparations. The tantalizing aroma of her chicken soup wafted through the air. I went into the kitchen to see if my help was needed.

"Rivky, do you like gefilte fish? I have a jar here and thought you'd like to take it," Mom said, looking at me fondly.

"Well, I don't really like gefilte fish, but you know what? Pack it up. Maybe I'll be in the mood for it."

"I have pastrami and turkey cold cuts," Mom continued. "How much should I pack for you?"

I thought for a moment and said, "I'll take the whole thing." Surprised at myself, I thought, *This is quite strange. How much could I possibly eat? A few slices of each would be more than adequate for me.* Again some inner voice told me to take extra; perhaps it would become necessary. Soon I was quite overloaded with coleslaw, salad, pickles, and more. I was sure that I had enough to feed at least three people, if not more.

Laibel drove me back to the nursing home. We rode quietly until Laibel's voice splintered the silence. "I've been learning the laws of mourning from the book *Mourning Halachos.* I brought it along for you. I think it's a good idea to be prepared and to learn the applicable halachos that we'll need, if and when the time comes. Of course, it's entirely up to the Almighty, but we should be knowledgeable."

I blinked back the tears. "Laibel, I began learning the halachos in Israel already. Yeshaya borrowed the same book for me and I've read most of it, though I'm still having a hard time accepting the situation."

We pulled up to the nursing home and hurried to Dad's room. Laibel gave Dad a kiss on the cheek and announced our arrival. Then he guided me out into the adjacent anteroom.

All of our food bags had been labeled. Laibel placed most of them into the refrigerator and helped me get settled. He'd been through this procedure many times before. As he handed me the book on the halachos of mourning, he added, "Rivkah, I doubt if it will happen to you while you are with Dad over Shabbos, but just in case, remember — you're not allowed to cry."

I interrupted with a gulp, "You mean — because it's Shabbos?"

He shook his head. "No, I mean anytime. I learned that if one cries out at the time that the *neshamah* leaves the body, it causes pain to the *neshamah* and it has to temporarily return to the body."

He continued, "I hope everything will go well with you, and may Hashem give you strength. By the way, I have a special signal with the nurses. If they need me on Shabbos, they can ring once, hang up, and ring again. I'll answer the phone."

Curious, I asked, "Did they ever contact you on Shabbos?"

"Yes, they once called me in Denver to tell me that Dad refused to take his medicine. We're talking about *pikuach nefesh*! I insisted that they put him on the line, and *baruch Hashem*, I was able to convince him to take the pills.

"I have to hurry now; I don't know what the traffic will be like on the way back. I'll call you right after Shabbos." With these closing words, he was on his way. I was left with a lump in my throat and a long road of uncertainty to travel, still not knowing what to expect.

CHAPTER 14

Flickering Light — *"Kulo Shabbos"*

I tried to push my dreary thoughts out of my mind and prepare myself for Shabbos. I was all alone, ready to experience my private Shabbos with my father.

For safety reasons small electric lights were lit for Shabbos instead of candles. Laibel had worked out in advance exactly what Jewish law permitted under the circumstances. I also knew that Shaya had lit candles for the whole family in Israel.

On Friday night — the sixth of Adar — I sat next to my father and sang the beautiful songs of *Kabbalas Shabbos*. I was confident that this not only gave me peace of mind, but gave it to my father as well.

The nurse entered to clear my father's passageways with what seemed to be a quick but painful procedure. He responded by tightening his lips with a slight jerk of his head. His doctor had warned me that if he didn't respond to this maneuver in an overt manner, it would be an indication of the deterioration of the situation — at its absolute end. As much as it hurt me to see him cringe in agony, I was relieved that he still responded.

A strained atmosphere permeated the room. The nurse touched his forehead. "I think he has some fever," she said softly.

I blew out a breath. "Is there anything that can be done about it?"

"I'll bring him some wet cool compresses and insert them under his arms and wherever necessary," she answered, hurrying out of the room.

She returned within a few minutes to attend to my father. I held his hand for a few moments; it was quite warm to the touch. "Daddy, it's Rivky, I'm here. I'll sing to you and we'll share Shabbos together," I said softly.

I listened to his shallow breathing. He must have been uncomfortable; if not for the heavy doses of morphine, he'd probably have been in unbearable pain. He didn't have enough strength in his waning body to give any response.

The doctor had taken him off the intravenous drip just a few hours earlier because he felt that the swelling was caused by overhydration; enough liquid remained in my father's body to keep him alive without the IV. Personally, I wasn't convinced. My concern was that, perhaps, by not getting any nourishment whatsoever, he could succumb to dehydration or a slow starvation. However, with my limited medical knowledge I had no choice but to heed the doctor's orders.

I davened *maariv* with as much *kavanah* as possible. Then we were ready for Kiddush. Pouring the grape juice into the silver-plated goblet made me think of all the Shabbosos we'd shared before I was married, when Dad would sing the Kiddush in the melody most familiar to him. I sang the tune that he always loved and, after drinking the required amount, placed some of the grape juice on his lips with my finger. He didn't show any significant response, but I felt that spiritually he was with me every moment.

I washed my hands and said *HaMotzi* over the challos Mom had so carefully packed for me. After consuming most of the *seudah*, I continued singing Shabbos *zemiros* with Dad, deliberately choosing his favorite melodies. The room was poorly lit; only the adjacent bathroom light was left on, yet it cast sufficient light on the words in my siddur.

Singing with all my heart, I felt the holiness of the Shabbos surrounding us. Suddenly, I glanced up from my siddur and saw Dad swaying back and forth. Then I heard his voice joining mine in the tune. I continued singing, wanting to pinch myself to see if I was dreaming. Something told me that even though I was overtired, this was very real.

Although no actual words emanated from his mouth, Dad was clearly singing one of the *zemiros* I sang in an "aye yi yi" fashion, rocking to and fro. His eyes seemed to bulge out of their sockets, covered by his almost transparent eyelids. His face was aglow. What was he seeing? I felt certain that he was seeing more than what I was able to see. He appeared to me as if he were *kulo Shabbos*. I could almost feel the *malachei hashareis* hovering over us in the room.

Our spiritual contact was interrupted when the floor nurse entered the room and said it was time to clean my father's mouth. I gripped my father's hand once again, but it was very cold to the touch. The fact sheet said that this indicated a warning — prior to the end. I thought to myself, *It's not the end; it's only the beginning.*

The body is mortal, but the soul is not. Gan Eden would put an end to his suffering in this world. Suffering also has its purpose, easing the way, in a sense, into Gan Eden. The burdens we carry on our shoulders in this world help to cancel out any sins we have committed. I offered a silent prayer, asking for Hashem to give me strength for whatever I might have to endure.

I moved to the foot of the bed to make room for the nurse. When she inserted the apparatus into his mouth, Dad did not respond. My heart seemed to skip a few beats, followed by a rapid thumping. I knew that I had to brace myself for the worst.

The nurse then took his pulse and said gently, "There isn't much of a pulse left."

I felt my stomach turn into one giant knot, but with a tremendous power I harnessed my tears. Ignoring my wildly beating heart, I began to recite aloud, "*Ana bekoach gedulas yemincha....*"

The nurse looked up at me and said softly, "There's no more pulse."

"*Shema Yisrael, Hashem Elokeinu, Hashem echad,*" I said out loud. Knowing I had to complete my mitzvah and uphold the Torah, I held myself together and did not allow a single tear to fall.

The nurse, looking at me in awe, said, "I'm so sorry. If there's anything we can do for you, please don't hesitate to ask."

Shaking, I opened the window and slowly moved closer to my father to cover his head with the white sheet. It was a very difficult moment, but I knew that only I could do what had to be done now.

Another night nurse approached me. "I'm so sorry. If there is anything that we can do for you, please let us know. I just want to tell you that your dad waited for you!"

My body was still quivering; my heart was pounding as if there was a hammer inside my chest, but I managed to briefly consult the mourning book and tell the nurse (without direct instructions because it was Shabbos), "It would be significant if my father's big toes were tied together with a piece of string."

With a peculiar look on her face, she answered automatically, "I'll take care of it immediately." She slowly backed out of the room and returned with some twine to do exactly what I had requested.

Suddenly, to my dismay, I remembered the signal that my brother had set up with the nurses' station. There would be no point in having them call him, as there was no longer a situation of *pikuach nefesh*. Although none of the nurses were Jewish, there would be a problem on my brother's end, having to answer the phone on Shabbos. By the time I told the nurses not to call, however, it was too late; Laibel had already been informed. I asked the nurse what he said, and she replied, "He let me know that he's coming."

"Anything else? Did he say when?" I asked anxiously.

"No, he just said he's coming. That's all."

Clutching my *sefer* on the halachos of mourning, I began to read all pertinent sections. As of *motza'ei Shabbos*, I would be considered an *onen*. Because it was Shabbos many of the laws did not apply at the moment. Pouring out the liquids in the room was also not applicable.

I had been "appointed" as my father's *shomeres*, since I was the only *shomer Shabbos* person in the vicinity. Until my brother arrived, this obligation rested solely on me.

I took out my precious, tear-stained *Tehillim* and poured out my heart in acceptance of Hashem's decree. My father's flame no longer burned in this world. The time had come to return his *neshamah* to his Maker. His mortal light had been extinguished; he would be going on to meet a greater light.

Our family would have to adjust to his absence. Gazing at his motionless body, a sense of helplessness overcame me, yet at the time I felt a sense of thankfulness. The One Above had chosen me to be with my father in his last moments on this earth. It is very special for a child to be able to say *Shema Yisrael* for a parent.

The fact that I had made it to Cleveland in the nick of time showed me how much Hashem is in charge of this world. The pieces of the puzzle were each fitting into place.

Tremors were still coursing through my body from the experience I'd just encountered, but gradually my eyelids began to droop. Before I knew it, sleep caught me in its mighty trap.

"Rivkah, we're here." The booming announcement pulled me out of my deep sleep, causing the palpitations in my chest to start again. For a moment, I wasn't sure where I was or what was happening, but when I saw my brother standing near me I remembered the dismal reality.

"Laibel, what time is it? Didn't it take you an awful long time to get here?" I asked.

Laibel, whose cheeks were as red as apples from the cold, said, "There's a blizzard out there! Avraham came to help."

Seeing the snowflakes scatter through the air after a quick glance out the window, I absorbed the truth of Laibel's words.

My brother's face contorted with pain as he took sight of my father's motionless body. After taking a long breath, he continued, "We went to consult with Rabbi Grumer a few pertinent halachic questions before coming here. It was a long walk in the blizzard. Believe me, I'm very thankful to be here now. I think we should take turns watching over Dad. We'll prepare some beds out in the hall and sleep in shifts."

I nodded in agreement, still too tired to think straight. "Laibel, I really feel terrible about falling asleep, but under the circumstances, it just happened."

"Don't worry about it. You were doing the best you could.

You had a huge responsibility resting on your shoulders, and I'm sure you handled it well. Do you feel like talking about what happened now?"

I described, very briefly, what I'd gone through and then said I preferred to save the rest of the details for the next day so I wouldn't totally collapse from fatigue.

We took turns sleeping and keeping the vigil throughout the night. Although my nephew, Avraham, was only sixteen and a half, he felt competent to participate in this mitzvah.

Morning dawned on the snow-laden city.

"Laibel, did you bring along any food?" I asked.

"Food? There's no *eiruv* here. I wasn't allowed to carry anything with me. We'll have to manage on what you brought."

It now dawned on me why I'd accepted such a large quantity of food. "You don't have to worry about a thing. I packed plenty of food, and it's unbelievable how even this particular detail was taken care of by the Ribbono shel Olam Himself." Another piece of the puzzle fit right into place.

Shabbos, March 15, 1997

The day passed quietly and the hospital staff hardly bothered us. When my brother and nephew returned from davening, Laibel made Kiddush and we all ritually washed our hands. The three of us shared the food I'd so "generously" brought and discussed the events of the preceding night.

As no preparations for the burial could be made on Shabbos, we knew that right after Havdalah we would have to get to work on the funeral arrangements. I thought back to when Laibel had discussed the place of burial with Dad. He told

us that he'd considered buying a plot near his mother and father. We asked him if he'd perhaps thought about Eretz Yisrael.
I had asked Rav Leff if it's more important for a person to be buried near his parents or in a place where his children can visit the
kever. "If a person has a chance to be buried in Eretz Yisrael, that
takes precedence over everything else," was his response.

When we presented this idea to Dad, he asked, "How far
would it be from Rivky?"

"We're talking about Beit Shemesh. It's about a half-hour
drive from Yerushalayim."

After contemplating the idea for a while, he decided,
"Okay, you can purchase a plot in Beit Shemesh. I guess if I can't
make it to Israel standing on my own two feet, I'll have to come
lying down in a box."

"Please, Dad, you should live and be well until 120. Did you
know that the purchase of a plot usually grants long life?"

"What about Mom?" Dad inquired.

"She'll buy the plot adjacent to yours," Laibel assured him.

"Time for Havdalah!" Laibel's announcement stirred me
back to reality. Avraham made Havdalah and drank the grape
juice (now prohibited to Laibel and myself). We were in the category of *onen* until the burial. All mitzvos except for taking care
of the *niftar* were prohibited to us.

My brother placed the important phone calls while I looked
on, almost envious of his ability to tackle the situation. I overheard him telling the *chevrah kaddisha*, "I think if anyone would
have tried to enter the room and removed the body, my sister
would have barred the door and prohibited entrance!"

I later found out that the policy in the hospitals and nursing homes is to remove the corpse within a very short time of

the death. This had been (in all likelihood) the first exception to the rule. I assume that the nurses were so awed over what had transpired that they didn't even think about doing anything against our wishes. To me, it was obviously the hand of Hashem extending honor to the deceased.

I remained with Dad's body while Laibel went to help with the *chevrah kaddisha*. I phoned Mom. In between sobs, she told me that having my sister-in-law, Sorah, by her side was a true consolation. "Sorah kept me calm — she was wonderful."

That night, sleep was long in coming. I tossed and turned in my old bed in Mom's house. The following morning, we'd be accompanying my father's body to the airport, from where he'd be flown to Israel.

CHAPTER 15

Mourning follows Morning

The funeral was to take place in Cleveland first, where Laibel would address the crowd coming to pay their last respects to my dearly beloved father. Rabbi Schur would also speak, and perhaps someone else who had been close to Dad. Seeing relatives I hadn't seen in years would present me with various problems in their own right. I knew I would do whatever I had to.

On Sunday morning, I awoke to the incessant ringing of the phone. I stayed in bed as long as I could. Even though I knew I had to face the world, I wasn't sure if I was ready for it. I already missed my father immensely.

Again the phone rang. "Rivkah, pick up the phone. It's Shaya!" Laibel shouted.

I looked at my watch; it read seven o'clock. That meant it was two o'clock in the afternoon in Israel. Yeshaya was anxiously waiting to talk to me.

Grasping the receiver, I began in a quivering voice, "Shaya, Dad's *neshamah* — has been returned to his Maker."

Our tears began to fall unchecked, and I heard him declaring, "*Baruch Dayan HaEmes.*"

After a moment of silence he continued, "Were you with

him when it happened?"

"Yes. It was the most unbelievable experience." The tears were still running down my face as I mustered my strength to relate the entire episode to my husband.

An eerie silence prevailed as we rode to the funeral parlor. The wind was still beating against the barren branches of the trees all around, refusing to allow the early spring buds to appear.

"March comes in like a lion and goes out like a lamb" is the popular saying. Although we'd just progressed into mid-March, the weather matched my melancholy mood. Intellectually I understood that Dad had moved on to a better place and would suffer no more, but I still found it difficult to adjust to this new situation.

Soon I would be returning to my family in Israel, but Mom would have to face the loneliness by herself. This in itself was enough to cause me grief. I was consoled by the knowledge that time would slowly heal the wound and Mom would find solace in turning to her Creator for support.

This was the first time I would be sitting shivah. I was still having misgivings as to whether or not I'd made the right decision the previous night. It had been resolved that Laibel would escort my father's body to Israel and be present at the Israel *levayah*. I'd always thought it would be me who would be there, as I lived in Eretz Yisrael while Laibel did not.

Before embarking on his role in the field of teaching, Laibel had asked his *rosh yeshivah* (of Telshe Yeshiva in Chicago, where he was studying in the *kollel*) if he should move to Israel. At the time, he was encouraged to go to teach in places where *Yiddishkeit* was lacking and he would be needed most. He moved to Phoenix, Arizona, where he became a most popular teacher. (I think that he was one of the only ones in the city who didn't own a television.) His next destination was Denver, Colorado. Again, he became a sought-after teacher, a beacon of Torah.

However, it would be proper for Laibel, as the only son, to speak and give a *hesped* on my father's behalf. Looking at my brother now, I realized that he was preparing for his talk, thinking of choice words to eulogize Dad. Laibel could speak quite well, and I was confident that he'd make all of us proud of him. He would need to make an impact, as most of my father's family in Cleveland was not religious.

The baby had been left with a babysitter, and my sister-in-law, Sorah, had time to collect her thoughts. She'd gone through this herself about a year earlier, when her mother had passed away. The loss of a parent definitely leaves a void.

Condolence can be offered for a full year to a person whose parent has passed on. One year of mourning can't compensate for the many years that a parent invests in his children's upbringing; however, it is the longest mourning period for any relative. A mourner's life changes drastically, as social activity virtually comes to a standstill.

An open book for all the "guests" to sign caught my eye as we entered the funeral home. It seemed strange to me, as this practice is nonexistent in Israel.

Reaching our respective places, we waited for the rabbi to begin the service. Glancing around, I caught sight of many familiar heads nodding in my direction. I'd been at other funerals, but this was the first one where I personally would be counted amongst the mourners.

Providence had arranged my arrival some years back in this same funeral parlor, for my Bubby Crystal's funeral. She passed away during a brief visit that I'd made to Cleveland. I was grateful for the opportunity to be with my father and console him at that time.

I couldn't help but ponder on how we have to be so thankful for whatever God gives and appreciate it while it lasts. (We say "*baruch Hashem*" for both the good and the seemingly bad. Everything that Hashem does is good, but sometimes this is not easily seen, making it difficult to grasp this concept.)

In this world no answers are given, but in the next world no questions are asked. The comprehension of Hashem's ways is beyond human capability, whereas acceptance of His will is within our reach. This does not mean that we should not do our utmost in *hishtadlus*. To the contrary, we need to make every possible effort in any given situation. Life is a gift. We must do our maximum to preserve it and make the most of our existence.

Rabbi Yisrael Salanter once observed a shoemaker working late into the night. He asked him, "Why are you working at such a late hour?"

The shoemaker responded, "As long as the candle continues to burn, I can still mend shoes."

Rav Salanter thought, *As long as the neshamah remains in the body, one can mend his ways.* From the example of this shoemaker, he understood that we should always be making efforts to improve ourselves.

Rabbi Schur was first to speak. He'd been my father's rabbi for decades (as well as the *mohel* at Laibel's bris). He cried through his beautiful speech, moving us to tears. I was thankful that I could release my pent-up feelings. The *rav's* moving words affected the entire crowd.

Rabbi Grumer was the next eloquent speaker, honoring our family with his eulogy of my father. We had attended the shul where he had served as the rabbi for many years.

Rabbi Ozbond, a *rosh yeshivah* of Cleveland Telshe, spoke next, relating various incidents of how my father had helped and supported the yeshivah. He offered rides to the various *rabbanim* and displayed a genuine respect for them. I remembered how my father cried at every *frum* wedding even before he'd become religious.

Laibel took the podium last. His whole body trembled as he gave his eulogy. Like the rabbis who spoke before him, he mentioned Dad's *mesiras nefesh* for the sake of Shabbos.

Yes, Dad had done everything for his children. He became *shomer Shabbos*, quit smoking, and dedicated his life to his children and grandchildren. In between his tears, Laibel expressed these ideas with sincere praises.

After the funeral, most of the crowd dispersed. The small entourage that remained escorted my father's body to the airfield.

Rebbetzin Schur helped my mother and I to *reis kriah* after we entered the cargo department. She urged us to sit on a stoop for a few minutes so we could begin our first day of shivah, as sundown was rapidly approaching.

The box carrying my father's body moved closer to the runway. Sobbing uncontrollably, with tears streaming down his chubby cheeks, my cousin Eric said, "I can't believe that Uncle Sammy is in that box!"

When Eric was born, his mother, my cousin Linda, had an extremely difficult birth. Forceps had been used, resulting in slight brain damage. Eric's physical and mental development was slow, but he was always a delightfully sweet child. When his father succumbed to the dreaded disease, his mother had to raise him on her own. My father had taken him under his wing, protecting and helping him whenever possible. Now Eric was crying like a baby for my father, his great-uncle. An important light in his life had been extinguished.

Laibel's departure to Israel postponed his seven-day mourning period (until the burial, his status was that of an *onen*). On the endless ride home, trees, buildings, and scenery all became a blur. I could have been ascending on the plane to Eretz Yisrael, but I'd made the decision to remain with my mother to mourn. I owed it to my father to let Laibel go.

The traditional round rolls and hard-boiled eggs awaited us at the house. All the mirrors had been covered with cloth and customary low chairs were available for the mourners. I personally chose to sit on the floor most of the time.

There were many laws and customs still to learn. The rabbi and the book I'd brought were quite helpful.

I realized that I'd made the correct decision when people began to relate to their memories of my father. With a notepad in hand, I asked for firsthand stories about Dad.

My cousin Linda, about my age, cried when she related the following story.

"When Eric turned twelve, we began calling various Conservative and Reform temples about arranging his bar mitzvah. The response was usually the same: 'No, I'm sorry he won't be able to have a bar mitzvah.'

"I was ready to give up when your dad came over and said, 'Of course Eric will have a bar mitzvah. There is absolutely no question about it!' With that he called Rabbi Schur from the Orthodox synagogue where he prayed and made all the necessary arrangements.

"Every week Uncle Sammy sat on the couch in our living room, while Eric said the *berachos* in the kitchen. I can almost hear your Dad shouting now, 'Eric, a little louder; I can't hear you.' This encouragement enabled Eric to reach his maximum potential in reciting the *berachos*. Thanks to your father, Eric had his bar mitzvah in the shul on time. Afterwards he attended more Orthodox Jewish classes, and it was all your father's initiative."

Each day presented new and fascinating accounts.

My cousin Bernie said, "Many years ago, your dad's car was in the driveway and someone asked to have it moved out of the way. I plunged into the task without asking his permission. As I pulled out of the driveway, the side of his blue Chevy was scratched considerably. Believe me, I was petrified. I could just imagine what I was in for.

"When your Dad came home and noticed the job I'd done on his car, he approached me, boring his eyes straight into mine. I was too scared to move. I waited for the blow that I rightfully deserved. All he said was, 'Bernie, you're too young to drive.' He didn't get mad or anything. With that, the subject was closed. Boy, was I ever thankful for not 'getting it.' He was really a swell guy!"

Bernie's wife, Recia, mentioned, "At the *pidyon haben* for my grandson, your dad showed up. He was given a *berachah*. We were so happy to have Uncle Sammy with us. He cared so much about everyone, but family events were the most meaningful to him; he did his utmost never to miss them."

Mr. Krainess had been a long-time friend of Dad, since they were affiliated with the same shul. "One time a few couples decided to go boating. Your dad and I were in a canoe when it tipped over. Your father lost his glasses and his watch, but he didn't let that ruin the fun spirit of the day. He didn't get angry at all. As a matter of fact, for as long as I knew him, he didn't criticize. He savored life and was a genuine person."

His son, Jonathon Krainess, a young man in his late teens, added, "To me, he was my 'Uncle Sam.' He never raised his voice in our sukkah, except when telling a joke. He seemed to be everyone's friend or 'uncle.' "

These words provided the comfort I sought.

Tuesday, March 18, 1997

Dad's friend Marty Gulko had a perpetually jovial personality. He had the ability to make people laugh in all circumstances. With a wide smile he announced, "Your father liked to play cards. Before he became religious, it was one of his favorite pastimes. After becoming Torah observant, he figured out a way to endure this activity in a 'kosher' way. What do you think he did?"

Slapping his knee and laughing, Marty continued, "He decided to make a fund-raising project out of the card playing. All proceeds to the shul!"

Sitting near Marty was another man, who chimed in, "He was also noted for contributing *tzedakah* in a hidden manner. He heard about a poor family that was lacking meat for Shabbos. Your father made a deal with the butcher. He offered to donate the meat to the family on a weekly basis, with one stipulation: they would never discover the source. He was really tops." Neither my mother nor I had ever heard about this incident.

"Your dad used to drive some of the women home from classes when our husbands couldn't come to get us. He really showed a special level of kindness," piped up Betty Hoffer, my mother's acquaintance.

Betty's mother, elderly Mrs. Wish, was a slender, grandmotherly woman with crow's feet around her eyes and thin gray hair. She made it her business to come to Mom's house to offer her condolences. "He always complimented me. Older ladies rarely get such compliments. He also had a wonderful sense of humor."

Mom told me, "He was concerned about your cousin Jay's children. Guiding them into our sukkah, he handed them a *lulav* and *esrog*. Ryan at first refused to place a yarmulke on his head and take the *lulav* and *esrog*, but he changed his mind after his sister performed the mitzvah. He repeated the *berachos* after Dad, and happily announced, 'We just shook the big lemon and the tree!' "

Dad's friend Howard Moskowitz, a stocky man sporting a baseball cap, contributed, "I always referred to him as 'Sam with a smile.' He never said anything bad about anyone. If someone tried to degrade another person, he would immediately change the subject in order to avoid *lashon hara*."

Mrs. Gottesman was a member of the shul my father had attended. Beaming, she told us, "My husband, may he rest in peace, used to help your father and encourage him to get an *aliyah* in shul on Shabbos morning after he became religious. He was embarrassed and he didn't want it, but my husband insisted and helped him until he felt comfortable enough to do it on his own. His inner desire was to grow in *Yiddishkeit*.

"He would come into the kosher bakery, where I worked on Thursday nights, always patient. Whenever there were other customers, he'd say that he was not in a rush and they could take their turns first. He was consistently considerate of others."

A tall, thin fellow with a black yarmulke, Yehuda Appel, a son of my parents' friends, said, "Mr. Crystal would give advice on every topic imaginable. People would say, 'Call Sam. He has a solution to just about any problem.' The minute he received the call, he was on his way."

Everyone mentioned his intense pride in his Torah-observant grandchildren. It was a topic Dad never ceased to discuss. My father was a rich man, indeed. His riches stemmed from his *frum* children and grandchildren, continuously performing mitzvos and learning Torah.

Every night I'd think about the day's events, taking time to reflect on the different stories and finding consolation when reviewing my notes on what people had said. It had been an excellent idea to copy down all the memories of my father. Due to this solace, my sleep was undisturbed.

Wednesday morning, March 19, 1997

My last day in Cleveland brought many more consolers. Mr. Kurt Kohr, Dad's fast friend for many decades, sat down to converse with me. "I knew your father way back when your brother, known then as Jerry, was a youngster playing ball in public school. Your little brother was not a real exemplary ball player, but your father never let on. Other fathers would yell and get all riled up when their sons played ball poorly, but not your Dad. Whether Jerry missed the ball when at bat or held an empty catcher's mitt, he'd say, 'It's okay, Jerry. Maybe next time,' without ever raising his voice. You could really learn character from a guy like him."

Rabbi Yechezkel Munk, a very dear adviser and friend to our family ever since my brother and I had become religious, said, "Your father served Hashem with *temimus*, and that is a very hard *middah* to come by." On the staff of the Telshe Yeshiva, which my brother had attended from high school, this unassuming rabbi, with his kind demeanor, had always given me inspiration throughout the years. When my father's sickness had peaked, Laibel and I had sought the advice of Rabbi Munk, who motivated us to encourage our father and never allow him to give up. A glimmer of hope alone can keep an individual going.

Rebbetzin Grumer, a long-standing family friend, summed up the discussion: "He lived a very successful life and was a true *ba'al teshuvah*."

I thought about how success could be measured in many different ways. I attended numerous *shiurim* where Rabbi Leff expounded on this particular topic. To many Americans, the word *success* is spelled with the dollar sign. Accumulation of dollars or material possessions — "adult toys" — is the focal point of their lives. For Torah observant people, success should be equivalent to how much Torah and how many mitzvos a person can accumulate during his lifetime. It is unfortunate that so many Jews have allowed the dollar sign to take over their lives.

Rabbi Leff once saw a man wearing a T-shirt with the slogan "The one with the most toys wins" printed on it. This person clearly had no awareness of the real goal in Jewish life, to amass as many spiritual assets as possible. I was happy to know that my father, with his own simplistic faith, had accumulated Torah and mitzvos; thus, he was able to leave this world with the praise that he had become a true *ba'al teshuvah*.

Rabbi Schur's wife, a modest woman always lending a helping hand in every way imaginable, came again to offer me solace before my return to Israel. "Your father always showed up at board meetings. He pushed for all positive religious legislation, as well as a raise in the rabbi's salary. He never hesitated to help out with shul functions or fund-raising dinners. He'd roll up his sleeves and help make the steaks; a fine chef he turned out to be." Tears began to well up in her eyes. My own vision clouded as well.

"The rabbi and I had constant *nachas* from him as he shared his delight in his children and grandchildren with us. He would always mention how he was perpetually doing it for them, but we knew he was also practicing everything for himself and *l'sheim Shamayim*. In my humble opinion, he portrayed real *gevurah*, a special strength."

Rebbetzin Schur went on to tell us of some of her family history. My mother and I sat spellbound as she related, "During the 1929 Chevron massacre, two of my brothers were learning in the Chevron Yeshivah. The day before the massacre, an Arab they were acquainted with told my brothers, 'Tell the *rosh yeshivah* not to let anyone come to the yeshivah tomorrow. Something very terrible is going to happen. If you want, I'll hide you.'

"My brothers did tell the *rosh yeshivah*, but he said he often received such warnings and it was just a bluff. Although the yeshivah had paid off the town sharif with high sums, Arabs were continually trying to banish the yeshivah.

"On the morning of the massacre, my two brothers, unsure if it was a false alarm, showed up at the Arab's place, where he ordered them urgently to hide beneath the donkey's manure. If they would be found, they would be killed, he warned, scared for himself as well. Reluctantly, they pushed their way under the putrid-smelling manure, remaining there for what seemed to be an endless amount of time. Suddenly, they heard voices. Someone shouted in Arabic, 'Traitor, are you hiding Jews?'

" 'No, certainly not!' replied my brothers' rescuer.

Unsheathing his sword, the attacker approached my brothers' hiding place and began to stab in every direction. The older of my two brothers, Zelig, received a stab in his back, piercing his kidney, but he didn't make a sound, knowing the slightest noise would mean absolute death. He kept his hand over the mouth of my younger brother, Azre'el, to make sure that no sound would escape. Azre'el, afflicted with a near fatal head wound, winced, but he too remained silent, enduring his pain gallantly."

All eyes in the room were focused intently on Rebbetzin Schur. She continued emotionally, "Before the bloodthirsty Arab left, he murdered my brothers' rescuer in cold blood, right in front of his poor wife. Finally, he ran from the premises, no doubt seeking more Jews to kill. The rescuer's shattered wife, in a state of near shock, courageously helped my brothers out of their hiding place and began to nurse their wounds. Whether her motive was pure or not, we'll probably never know, but the fact that she took care of my brothers was an expression of Hashem's mercy on our family.

"Chevron families had been torn apart; the devastation was beyond belief. Yeshivah students had been ruthlessly murdered in cold blood. Survivors were missing limbs or were left with remnants of their mutilated body parts. The Arabs had used swords and axes to vent their anger on innocent Jews — men, women, and children.

"My brothers were sent to a hospital in England for recuperation. An operation was not even a choice, and kidney dialysis was nonexistent. My younger brother developed migraine headaches from his severe injury and suffered from this condition for the rest of his life. Doctors told my older brother that he'd have a maximum of ten years to live. They both returned to the United States.

"Zelig spurned any thought of marriage. Although shiduchim were offered, he refused them, saying that it would be unfair for a wife to have a husband who would only live another ten years.

"There were very few serious young men learning in the

yeshivah in those days, and my brother was the cream of the crop. One special young lady told my mother that she preferred to be married for a short time to a *talmid chacham* than for many years to a plain *ba'al habayis*. Although my brother had his reservations, she refused to take no for an answer. They were married and lived happily together for the next thirteen years. Fulfilling the mitzvah of *peru u'revu*, they were blessed with a son and a daughter.

"The *gevurah* that my sister-in-law showed under the circumstances was exceptional," Rebbetzin Schur concluded. "My brothers related this entire episode to me when I was a young girl."

I called the airline company to change my flight. For the international flight I had no problem whatsoever. When I phoned Continental Airlines to switch my domestic flight, however, things did not go as smoothly. "What do you mean I have to come down personally to change it? I changed my international ticket without encountering any difficulty at all — a phone call and finished."

"That's the company policy. Sorry, ma'am, but you have no choice," I was told on no uncertain terms.

"Perhaps the company can make an exception this one time. You see, I am in a seven-day mourning period after the loss of my father; it is not appropriate for me to come."

"Listen, lady, rules are rules. If you want to change your ticket, you'll just have to show up like everyone else and that's all! Now I'm quite busy with other clients, so good day." With that she hung up, leaving me shaking my head is disbelief.

I phoned Rabbi Schur to ask what I was allowed to do under the circumstances. He advised me to go to the airport with my slippers on and then put on my shoes after alighting from the car. I should put some dirt in my shoes before I left the house. Equipped with everything, I was driven to the airport by a friend of the family.

The line was short and in almost no time I was speaking to the ticketing department. The woman took care of my changed ticket and said, "That will be fifty dollars, please."

I explained, "Madam, my father passed away and I therefore have to change my ticket. I don't see why this would require an additional payment. Here's the letter from the officiating doctor."

After a brief survey of the form I handed to her, she said unbendingly, "Only if you die would we be allowed to waive the charge."

Flabbergasted, I retaliated, "If that would be the case, I wouldn't have to change my ticket. I'd like to speak to your supervisor, please."

"She won't be available to speak to you directly. I'll try to talk to her, but I don't' think it will make any difference." With that, she left her desk.

I waited, thinking wistfully, *If I have to forfeit this money for any reason, may it not be a contribution to Continental Airlines. When I return to Israel, I'll use this money for the elevation of my father's neshamah. I would like to buy books for the children who will say mishnayos in his memory.*

The second that I finished my thought, the ticketing agent returned with an amazed look on her face. "It was approved," she said. I knew that it was Hashem who had approved of my alternative plan for this fifty dollars, and I offered Him my silent prayer of thanks. Although fifty dollars is not such an outstanding figure, I felt it could be better used for a mitzvah.

Returning to the *beis aveilim,* I related what had occurred at the airport and everyone was astonished. Even in this instance, I could see the hand of Hashem, and noted that another piece of the puzzle had been put into place.

CHAPTER 16

Final Destination

Thursday, March 20, 1997

With tears in my eyes, I kissed my mother good-bye. Although my brother and I had been able to sit shivah together for only half a day, my departure time had arrived. Laibel, who had pulled in a few hours earlier, filled me in on details of the funeral in Israel. It was difficult to leave him, since we did not see each other often, but my family eagerly awaited my return.

The house was still packed with visitors when I left. I took one last look at the house and at the name "Crystal" inscribed on the antique sign hanging from the tall gas lamppost before we pulled away. Fond memories filled my thoughts, accompanied by conflicting emotions. My past was buried in this little red brick house.

Engines roaring, the plane took off. We rose higher and higher until we were above the clouds and the "fasten seat belts" sign was turned off, enabling the passengers to relax. The tension I'd experienced on the in-coming trip was, *baruch Hashem*, gone on the return flight. I slept whenever possible to prepare for meeting my family and the comforters who would come to my home.

My husband came to pick me up at the airport alone, deciding it would be inappropriate to have the children come to greet me with pomp and fanfare (as many family members had been received in the past). After depositing my bag in the rear of the van, I spoke a bit about my various experiences. Yeshaya listened attentively. When I was too tired to talk anymore, I just sat quietly enjoying the breeze along the highway until we approached our building on Chazon Ish Street.

I dragged my tired body up the stairs, making a supreme effort to greet my children as cheerfully as possible. They were happy to see their mother, but sad to watch me sitting down on the low chair. Just two days before, they had seen their Uncle Laibel sit on the same small stool, so they were already aware of the custom.

The white, seven-day candle was still burning, but it had already burned quite low. The prayer services would not to be held in our home, as no male mourners were present. When Yeshaya went to daven *maariv*, I gave my children my undivided attention, sharing different experiences with them on a level that they could grasp. Fortunately, no visitors came during this time span.

We openly discussed the idea of a soul being returned to its Maker. Rachayli, her blue eyes shining, asked me, "Is Saba with Hashem now? Is he in Shamayim? Does that mean we can't see him anymore, and he won't come to us again with Savta for Pesach?"

With misty eyes, I managed to answer, "Yes, darling, everything you said is correct. It is not sad for Saba now. He is in Gan Eden, in a very good place. It's only sad for us, because we won't be able to see him anymore. This time Savta will be coming alone for Pesach."

Moishy asked solemnly, "Were my *tefillos* said in vain?"

I reassured him, "No *tefillos* are said for naught. All prayers reach Shamayim, but the Ribbono shel Olam decides when, how, or for whom to use them." I then related the incident of a Telshe *rosh yeshivah*'s wife, which I had heard in a *shiur* given by Rav Leff.

"A round-the-clock *Tehillim* schedule had been in effect for a number of days for the ailing *rosh yeshivah*. When the news broke that the *rosh yeshivah* had passed away, in spite of the vigil that had been kept for him, one *bachur* was extremely forlorn.

"He approached the *rebbetzin* during the shivah and said that his supplications were useless. The *rebbetzin* answered, '*Chas veshalom*, don't ever say or even think that. Hashem discerns how to utilize our prayers. Don't think for a moment that your *tefillos* were not used or accepted. Every one of the yeshivah students who spent their free hours saying *Tehillim* spent their time wisely. HaKadosh Baruch Hu saves and stores the precious prayers and tears. They are put to use where and when they are most needed. It was the appointed time for my husband, the *rosh yeshivah*, to return his pure soul to his Maker, but your *tefillos* were needed, obviously for a different reason. Please remember this lesson and continue to say *Tehillim* for *klal Yisrael*.' Children, remember this lesson well."

On Friday morning, I finished my shivah period. Although relieved to be with my own family for Shabbos, an eerie feeling filled me. Just one week earlier, I was spending Shabbos with my father, *alav hashalom*.

It would take time to absorb the new situation. A child is in the state of *aveilus* for an entire year. For this duration, he must refrain from attending all *simchah*s, purchasing new clothes, listening to music, and cutting his hair (for men — three months,

or until people let him know it's too long). There are many laws
that apply to the mourning period, and when it becomes applicable, we delve into them to better understand what is expected
of us.

I knew that it would be a difficult year for me, as I am a very
outgoing person and enjoy participating in the *simchah*s of my
friends. I was not one to buy clothes that often; however, knowing that I wasn't not allowed to buy them made the *yetzer hara*
greater and the desire to purchase them immense. I knew that
I'd manage, because all along the way I'd be giving constant
honor to my father.

My mother came for Pesach. It seemed very strange not to
have Saba there to join in the joy of Pesach.

During the month of Nissan, it is customary not to go to
cemeteries. We therefore attended the stone setting in the *beis
hakevaros* Eretz HaChaim in Beit Shemesh in Iyar. *Tehillim* were
recited, and some words of Torah were spoken in memory of my
father. On his tombstone it says, in Hebrew:

Ish tam v'tuv lev
Ahuv l'beriyos v'osan aheiv
Ba'al chesed v'shem tov
B'nei Torah tze'etza'av larov.
Yad Hashem ra'ah b'ma'asav
Nasa b'gvurah yesurav.
Al shemiras Shabbos masar nafsho
Uv'Shabbas Kodesh hechzir neshmaso.
Nolad Tu B'Shvat Tarpaz
Nelb"a Vav Adar Tashnaz
Tntb"h

Free translation:

A simple man with a good heart
Loved people and for them did his part.
Extending kindness with an exemplary good name,
Rewarded with grandchildren who learn Torah
as their claim to fame.
Constantly seeing the hand of Hashem in every way,
Accepting his suffering with inner strength,
not a word did he say.
Sacrificing for the sake of Shabbos, never a taker,
On Shabbos Kodesh he returned his soul to his Maker.
Born 15 Shevat, 5687
Died 6 Adar, 5757

The puzzle seemed to have been completed; however, Hashem's puzzles are forever undergoing changes.

CHAPTER 17

Returning to the Kosel

Rosh Chodesh Elul, 1999

I have been to the Kosel HaMaaravi many times to daven since my father's passing, but this particular visit with my children and grandson demands mention. The boys walked to the men's side of the *mechitzah* to daven with my husband, while I took the girls and my grandson with me to the women's section.

Although the air had only a slight chill to it, I remembered the cold dreary day when I'd brought the children to daven for my father prior to his operation over five years before. Shivering, we had stood davening with as much concentration as possible. Now we stood huddling close together on Rosh Chodesh Elul. The blackness of night had descended upon the praying crowds, but it almost seemed as if light was flickering on the Wall, illuminating every woman deep in her own special, heartrending *tefillah*.

We inched our way forward, taking *sifrei Tehillim* from the table in the center and then finding a small opening amid the many women. My girls and my four-year-old grandson squeezed through and planted kisses on the cherished Western

Wall. Chani opened her *Tehillim* diligently, softly and slowly enunciating every word of the first chapter. Rachayli pulled out a siddur to daven *Shemoneh Esrei*, while Miryam held her *Sefer Tehillim* with half-closed eyes, concentrating on the words with her full heart. It was a most endearing scene. We had spoken about the significance of the month of Elul and how we must ready ourselves for the Days of Awe — Rosh HaShanah and Yom Kippur. The seriousness of the Jewish people during this month would play a major part in the decisions that would be made on High by HaKadosh Baruch Hu for individuals and for *am Yisrael*.

I sat down on an available chair to recite *tehillim*. My little grandson, absorbing all that was going on around him, suddenly blurted out, "Bubby, I want to sit on your lap!"

This was truly a "*chiddush*," as he rarely, if ever, asked to sit on my lap. With a big smile, I pulled him up onto my lap.

His big brown eyes watched intensely as I continued to say *Tehillim*, until he asked to use my *Sefer Tehillim*. "Bubby, I want to say *alef beis*." He began to pronounce every letter of the first three lines, keeping the place with his finger. He seemed to know them quite well and he radiated pleasure when I complimented him. Once he made a mistake and asked, "Is this a *tzaddi*?"

I responded, "No, *motek*, it's an *ayin*."

When he finished he said, "That's all," and climbed down.

I thought to myself, *What a beautiful way to offer his prayer to the Ribbono shel Olam — in the only way he knew how.* I was quite sure his special *tefillah*, expressed so meaningfully, went straight up to Shamayim. I thought, *My dear Daddy, I'm sure that your coat of mitzvos is growing daily from your precious grandchildren and great-grandchildren.*

EPILOGUE

October 25, 2000

Returning to Cleveland to pack my mother's belongings for her imminent aliyah to Israel was imperative. When my newly married daughter Sari and her husband Moishe generously offered to stay in our house and watch the children, my husband, Miryam, and I resolved to make the trip.

Once in Cleveland, we boarded the bus to the rental car companies. Engaging in a conversation with some other "members of the tribe" (noticeably Jewish passengers), my husband and I said, "It's our daughter's first time in America."

"Her first time in the U.S., and you bring her to Cleveland?" the man asked in bewilderment.

Miryam giggled. "We brought her to visit her grandmother and attend her cousin's wedding," I chuckled.

Comprehending, he nodded his head. "Now I see."

In addition to helping Mom, we attended my husband's nephew's wedding. The *chasunah* took place in the Taylor Road Synagogue conveniently located right next to Cane Park. The *chuppah* was held outdoors under the stars. Beautiful, multicolored leaves covered the ground in all directions, and the weather was compliant on this perfect fall evening. Landing in an enchanted forest, I felt like I was reliving the past.

The Telshe *rosh yeshivah*, Rav Ozbond, was *mesader kiddushin*. Twenty-six years and a half years before, he had been the *mesader kiddushin* under my own *chuppah*. Rav Grumer, well known and respected as the "rabbi's rabbi" for exceptionally difficult *shailos*, was blessing the new couple. He, too, had recited a *berachah* under my *chuppah*.

His charming wife looked as if she hadn't aged a day over the last two and a half decades. "Rivkah," she whispered, "it's hard to believe, but my husband is a walking miracle. A few weeks ago, on Shabbos morning, while he was taking the three steps back at the end of *Shemoneh Esrei*, he collapsed."

I gasped, but Rebbetzin Grumer continued calmly, "It was unbelievable *hashgachah* that a doctor who was scheduled to daven in a different shul was present among the worshipers. He sprinted immediately to my husband and administered artificial respiration. One of the shul members tried to get into the office to telephone an ambulance, but the door was locked because it was Shabbos. Someone finally reached the emergency squad, but *baruch Hashem*, the doctor in our minyan had been sent to help keep the rabbi alive.

"Shock was administered and it was effective for a while, but he fainted again. Fortunately, the Almighty helped and he was ushered into the emergency room of the hospital, where he had to undergo a quadruple bypass operation on his heart. One of the doctors, astonished at the successful outcome of the operation, commented, 'Rabbi, someone must be watching over you from up there!' "

She concluded, "Today you are witnessing a miracle — my

husband reciting this *berachah* at the wedding ceremony."

With awe, I looked over to where Rabbi Grumer stood under the *chuppah*. Hashem should bless him to continue to spread Torah in the world.

Vibrant song and dance filled the wedding hall, bringing joy to the newly married couple. *Yeshivah bachurim* carrying the groom, his father, and father-in-law on their shoulders spun round and round, captivating their audience. Everyone joined in the mitzvah of entertaining the *chasan* and *kallah*, who entered a new era of their life.

During the next few days, we looked over all the old papers and packed. After throwing out approximately one hundred giant plastic bags of garbage, we had nearly completed our task. Shabbos was a welcome respite, and the *sheva berachos* served to weave the family together.

Motza'ei Shabbos was designated for a visit to my father's only remaining sister. I gathered my emotional strength to make the trip to the Montefiore Nursing Home, where Dad resided until his passing. The corridor, lined with pictures, hadn't changed; it brought back memories of my last visit to my father.

As we approached my Aunt Rose's bed, the pungent hospital smells revived my queasy feelings. I overcame my feelings and smiled at my sick aunt. "Hi, Aunt Rose! You look pretty good. Meet my daughter, Miryam. It's her first visit to the States."

"I'm really happy to meet you," Miryam said. "I've heard so much about you, and I've seen you in the family picture albums."

Flattered, my aunt told her, "You don't even have an Israeli accent. If I didn't know better, I would have thought you were

American born. It's so wonderful to see all of you. You can't imagine what it does for a person like me to have visitors all the way from Israel!"

Her eyes on me, she continued, "Rivky, I have to tell you something that I can never forget."

Not knowing what to expect, I asked, "What is it?"

"You know your father and I were very close. Sammy was the youngest in the family, less than two years younger than I. We were almost like twins. Your father and I tried to stay out of trouble, but whenever Uncle Jack found we'd done something wrong, he'd put us in corners on opposite sides of the room, warning us not to come out until he said so. We were so scared that we remained immobilized like statues long after Jack had left, and didn't even realize that the coast was clear.

"We grew up together and shared in everything. Being poor didn't take the fun out of life.

"We remained close even after we'd both married and had families of our own. Your Dad was a family-oriented person and never missed a 'relatives outing' or *simchah*. After I'd lost my dear husband, Uncle Al, your father always came to check on me. If I needed groceries, bakery goods, or whatever, he'd be sure to pick them up for me. He would come to visit on a regular basis."

Catching her breath, she continued, "It was so bitter for me when my son, Barry, passed away. The fatal illness that took my son had also taken my son-in-law many years ago. Barry was such a good and considerate son. Your Dad helped with everything, including a proper funeral, and made sure I was taken care of. He always brought over extra chicken, cholent, cakes, and more. He or your mom would call before they'd go shopping to see if I needed anything. I could never forget all your father's kindness."

Whimpering, she continued, "Last year when my Linda'le left for the next world, it was too much for me to bear — I was heartbroken. Your father was no longer here for me to rely on, and I was already in this nursing home. Jay, the only son I have left, came to visit and did whatever he could for me. I'm thankful that he still comes often."

Pulling some tissues out of the nearest box, I handed some to her and dabbed my own eyes.

"When Jay came to tell me the news about your father, it didn't come as a total shock. I was prepared. Listen to the reason!

"I'll never forget it. It happened on that Friday night; I was resting when I saw a shadow in the room. Startled, I called, "Who's there?"

" 'Don't you recognize me? I'm your brother Sammy!'

"Just at that moment, the nurse walked in and asked, 'To whom are you speaking, Mrs. Friedberg?'

" 'Oh, it's nothing,' I told her. I fell asleep with heaviness on my heart.

"When Jay came into the room on Sunday, he said quietly, 'Mom, I have some bad news to tell you.'

"I didn't let him finish. I burst out, 'Sammy, my brother Sammy, I know it's Sammy. Right?'

"Jay was surprised that I knew, but the truth is that your father spared me the shock by coming to let me know that Friday night!"

We had certainly heard an earful! Even after his soul had departed, it seems that my father still took care of his sister. Hashem, in His abundant kindness, allowed my aunt to be informed of the unpleasant news in the easiest possible way.

After Yeshaya and Miryam left, Laibel and I continued cleaning up the house. We knew that Mom was a saver, but this proved to be quite funny. "Rivkah, take a guess at the date of the paid gas bill I've just discovered," Laibel chuckled.

"I don't know. Tell me."

"Go ahead and just take a guess."

"1975?"

"Try again."

"1970?"

"Nope, I think it qualifies as an antique; this old bill is dated March 1956!"

Laibel and I laughed until tears streamed down our faces. We worked fastidiously organizing Mom's possessions until Laibel had to depart.

I had a chance to bond with Mom when we shopped and drove to the cemeteries to daven by the *kevarim* of my grandparents. An uneasy feeling settled in my stomach when I realized that this might be my last time in Cleveland. With my bags packed, I kissed Mom good-bye and headed out to the airport to return the rented car. Although Mom had wanted me to stay another day, I had to go to New York to attend the *sheva berachos* of my husband's nephew and reunite with my daughter Miryam.

Stopping at the gas station was an experience. I had never filled gas with a pump before and relied on Laibel's instructions. Dressed in a new beige leather skirt, brown suede jacket, and Shabbos shoes, since I was planning to go straight from the airport to the *sheva berachos*, I hoped that none of the gas would spill onto my outfit.

I watched the slight elderly ladies with their thinning white hair pumping gas with ease. With no other option, I tried my luck, but soon discovered that gas pumping was not as simple as

I thought. After a few frustrating failures, I finally managed to fill the tank and exit from the gas station.

The cars on the highway were moving rapidly and I assumed I'd be at the airport in less than forty minutes. The trip usually takes between twenty-five and forty minutes. Speeding ahead at about sixty-five miles an hour, I turned on the radio to listen to the traffic news bulletin. The newscaster reported a heavy traffic backup due to an accident on the highway I was driving on. Before I knew it, I was caught up in the snarl.

Driving along at a speed of five to ten miles an hour, I realized that my chances of making the flight were becoming slimmer and slimmer. I decided to put my trust in HaKadosh Baruch Hu — whatever the outcome would be, I would accept His will.

Pulling up at curb-side checkin an hour and a half later, I begged for quick processing as my flight was due to depart in fifteen minutes.

"No, ma'am. You gotta return that car, and there ain't no way you gonna make it, but let's see what they say." The stocky black Continental employee escorted me into the building and pointed me in the right direction.

Behind the receiving desk stood a friendly looking woman in her mid-thirties. Looking at my ticket she politely said, "I'm very sorry, Mrs. Jacobs, but the flight is scheduled to leave at 5:45 promptly, so I'll have to transfer you to a later flight."

She added, "Don't worry, I'll make sure that your luggage gets onto the correct flight."

I was a bit leery about having my luggage transferred, since I had lost my luggage on three different trips to America, but with little choice I agreed. After she changed the documents, I rushed out to the car, where I'd left the keys in the ignition. Fortunately, it was still there, with all my belongings inside.

I drove slowly to the car rental return. An attendant motioned to me to pull over so he could check the mileage and gas gauge.

"Hey, lady, you been to California or somefin'?" he asked in disbelief, after reading the odometer below the dashboard.

"I only made a few trips to the airport and traveled locally in the Cleveland suburbs," I retorted.

"I guess they's a mistake here. Your gas ain't been filled up either, ma'am."

After all the trouble I'd been through to fill up the tank, it seemed I had made a blunder after all. Disappointed, I told the attendant, "I filled it up right before I came to the airport, but it was my first time using a gas pump."

The gangly attendant felt sorry for me. "Okay, lady, don't worry about it. It's full enough." He signed the papers and whisked me off to the desk to pay the bill.

I boarded the shuttle bus for the return ride to the airport, but I was in no hurry. My newly scheduled flight was not due to take off for at least another hour.

I strolled into the airline lobby and looked indifferently at the screen of arrivals and departures. To my surprise, my original flight had been exceedingly delayed. I hurried over to the agent at the counter and asked her if I could get onto that flight again.

"No problem. Just give me your ticket and I.D. and I'll readjust your ticket."

Before long everything was arranged, including my luggage. As I walked to the gate from which my flight was due to depart, I realized that I should have accepted the food my mother wanted me to take along. I had thought it unnecessary, as I'd soon be partaking of a festive meal at the *sheva berachos*. With my stomach growling, I looked at all the *treif* food counters in their abundance and pitied myself for not heeding my mother's words of wisdom.

I phoned my mother quickly. "Mom, how is everything now that I'm not with you?"

"Rivky, have you arrived in New York?" she answered my question with one of her own.

"No, Mom, I'm still in the Cleveland Hopkins Airport."

"What?! What happened?"

I briefly gave a rundown of the events I'd experienced and concluded, "Mom, everything is *bashert* and if I don't make the *sheva berachos*, then it just wasn't meant to be."

In HaKadosh Baruch Hu's grand puzzle, we can't always understand the "whys," but we just have to believe that everything is done for the good and certainly for our benefit.

Boarding time finally arrived. I found my seat easily because the plane was only half-full. I looked out the window as the plane took off, blinking back tears. This probably meant a real and final good-bye. Mom would be coming to live in Israel soon, *b'ezras Hashem*, and I doubted if I'd ever have any reason to return to this city of my childhood. It was a strange feeling.

As we climbed higher and higher, the houses looked smaller and smaller, and all of my Cleveland memories were becoming a part of my past. This particular part of the puzzle seemed to have been completed.

Glossary

All terms are Hebrew unless stated otherwise.

A

Adar — Hebrew month usually corresponding to February

a grosse danke schoine (Yid.) — thank you very much

akeidas Yitzchak — binding of Isaac

alav hashalom — may he rest in peace

alef beis — the Hebrew alphabet

aliyah — lit. "to go up," coming to live in Israel or being called up to recite the blessings over the Torah

amein — Amen (recited upon hearing a blessing)

am Yisrael — the nation of Israel

aveilus — mourning

Avinu — our Father (refers to God)

B

ba'al habayis — head of house; one who works for a living

ba'al teshuvah — one who has returned to Torah observance

bachur (pl. *bachurim*) — youth

Baruch Dayan HaEmes — "Blessed be the True Judge" (blessing pronounced on hearing of a death)

baruch Hashem — thank God

bashert (Yid.) — predestined; predestined mate

bas Yisrael — daughter of Israel

bein adam laMakom — between man and his Creator

bein adam l'chaveiro — between man and his fellowman

bein hazemanim — vacation time in yeshivos

beis aveilim — house of mourning

Beis HaMikdash — the Holy Temple

beis midrash — study hall

ben — son (of)

ben bayis — young man who is a regular visitor in a home

benched licht (Yid.) — lit candles (to inaugurate the Sabbath or a holiday)

bench gomel — to recite a blessing of thankfulness on being saved from death

ben zekunim — son of old age (one's youngest son)

berachah (pl. *berachos*) — blessing

b'ezras Hashem — with Hashem's help

bikur cholim — visiting the sick

Birkas HaGomel — blessing recited upon being saved from death

bris — ritual circumcision

Bubby (Yid.) — grandmother

C

chag — holiday

challah — braided bread eaten on Sabbath and holidays

chametz — leavening (refers to any bread or byproduct forbidden on Passover)

chasunah — wedding

chas vechalilah — God forbid

chas veshalom — God forbid

chesed — kindness

chevrah kaddisha — burial society

chiddush — a new understanding in Torah learning

chizuk — strengthening

cholent (Yid.) — hot dish served for the Sabbath morning meal

Chol HaMoed — intermediate days of the Passover and Sukkos holidays

chuppah — wedding ceremony

D

daf — page

daven (Yid.) — pray

divrei Torah — words of Torah

E

eiruv — enclosure which allows one to carry in a public domain on the Sabbath

eishes chayil — woman of valor

Elul — Hebrew month usually corresponding to September

Eretz Yisrael — the land of Israel

erev — the day prior to

esrog — citrus fruit used ceremonially on the Sukkos holiday

F

frum (Yid.) — religious

G

Gan Eden — Garden of Eden (refers to the World to Come)

gashmius — materialism

geveret — Mrs.

gevurah — strength

goyim — non-Jews

H

Ha'azinu — a portion (parashah) of the Five Books of Moses *hachnasas orchim* — welcoming guests

HaKadosh Baruch Hu — the Holy One, Blessed be He (God)

halachah (pl. halachos) — Torah laws

halachic — pertaining to Torah laws

HaMotzi — blessing on bread

Hashem — God

hashgachah — (Divine) providence

hashgachah peratis — Divine providence

Havdalah — ceremony performed at the conclusion of the Sabbath

hesped — eulogy

hishtadlus — making an attempt

hoda'ah — thanks

I̲

Ima — Mom

K̲

Kabbalas Shabbos — psalms recited to welcome the Sabbath

Kaddish — prayer of sanctification (in most cases recited in memory of a deceased)

kallah — bride

kashrus — Jewish dietary observances

kavanah — concentration

kedushah — holiness

kefitzas haderech — getting to a place faster than normal

kever (pl. *kevarim*) — grave

kibbud av va'eim — honoring one's father and mother

Kiddush — blessing recited over wine to sanctify the Sabbath and holidays

klal Yisrael — people of Israel

kollel — yeshivah for married men

Kosel or Kotel (HaMaaravi) — the Western Wall

kuchen (Yid.) — a sweet yeast cake with nuts

kulo Shabbos — completely Sabbath
kvell (Yid.) — feel intense pride

L

lashon hara — gossip
lehitraot — see you again
leichter (Yid.) — candelabra
leining (Yid.) — reading
levayah — funeral
l'sheim Shamayim — for the sake of Heaven
lulav — palm branch used ceremonially on the Sukkos holiday

M

maariv — evening prayer service
ma'aser — a tenth of one's income given to charity
ma'asros — tithes separated from produce grown in Israel and
    given to Levites
malach — angel
malachei hashareis — angels of glory
mara d'asra — rabbi
Mashiach — the Messiah
mechitzah — partition
mesader kiddushin — officiating rabbi at a wedding ceremony
mesiras nefesh — self-sacrifice
middah — characteristics
mikveh — ritual pool used for purification
minchah — afternoon prayer service
minyan — quorum of ten men
mishnayos — the earliest codification of Jewish oral law by Rabbi
    Yehudah HaNasi
Modeh Ani — prayer recited upon awakening
mohel — one who performs ritual circumcision

moshav shitufi — partially collective settlement

motek — sweetie

motza'ei Shabbos — Saturday night

N

nachas — joy

neshamah — soul

nesi'im — leaders of the tribes of Israel

niftar — deceased

Nissan — Hebrew month usually corresponding to March

nun — Hebrew letter corresponding to N

O

oleh (pl. *olim*) — one who has made aliyah

oneg — pleasure

onen — one whose close relative has died and has not yet been
   buried

P

parashah — weekly portion of the Torah

peru u'revu — be fruitful and multiply

Pesach — holiday of Passover

Pesachdik (Yid.) — items used only for Passover

pidyon haben — redeeming of the firstborn son

pikuach nefesh — saving a life

pirsum hanes — publicizing the miracle

pruste goyim (Yid.) — plain gentiles

R

rabbeinu — our teacher

rachmanus — mercy

rav — rabbi

rebbe (Yid.) — teacher; chassidic leader

rebbetzin (Yid.) — wife of a rabbi

refuah sheleimah — complete recovery

reis kriah (Yid.) — tearing of one's garments (in mourning)

Ribbono shel Olam — Master of the Universe (refers to God)

Rosh Chodesh — first day of the Hebrew month

rosh yeshivah (pl. *roshei yeshivah*) — head of a yeshivah

ruchnius — spirituality

S

Saba — Grandfather

sandek — the one who holds the infant during the circumcision

Sanhedrin — group of Rabbis who held court in the time of the Temple

Savta — Grandmother

seder — the ritual followed on the first night of Passover

sefer (pl. *sefarim*) — book

sefer Torah — Torah scroll

seudah — meal, especially a festive or Sabbath meal

seudas hoda'ah — meal of thanksgiving

Shabbos — Sabbath

shacharis — morning prayer service

shailos — questions (generally refers to questions pertaining to Torah law)

shalom zachor — a gathering in honor of a newborn baby boy on the first Friday night after his birth

Shamayim — Heaven

sheitel (Yid.) — wig

Shema Yisrael, Hashem Elokeinu, Hashem echad — Hear, O Israel, the Lord is our God, the Lord is One

shemittah — the seventh year in a seven-year cycle during which it is prohibited to work the Land in Israel

Shemoneh Esrei — the silent prayer of eighteen benedictions recited three times a day *sheva berachos* — seven benedictions recited under the wedding canopy and at every festive meal for seven days after the wedding

shidduch (pl. *shidduchim*) — match; refers to a potential marital partner

shiur — lecture

shivah — lit., seven; the seven-day mourning period following a death

shlep (Yid.) — to drag

shofar — ram's horn blown on the holiday of Rosh HaShanah

shomer, shomeres — guard

shomer Shabbos — Sabbath observer

shul (Yid.) — synagogue

siddur — prayer book

sifrei kodesh — Torah books

simchah — lit., joy; celebration

Sivan — Hebrew month corresponding to May or June

siyatta diShmaya — heavenly assistance

sukkah — temporary dwelling which is a central requirement of the Sukkos holiday

Sukkos — Jewish holiday celebrated in the fall

T

talmid — student

talmid chacham — Torah scholar

techiyas hameisim — resurrection of the dead

tefillah (pl. *tefillos*) — prayer, prayer service

Tefillas HaDerech — prayer recited when embarking on a journey

tefillin — phylacteries

Tehillim — psalms, book of Psalms

temimus — purity

terumah — tithes separated from produce grown in Eretz Yisrael and given to the priests *teshuvah* — repentance

tinokos shel beis rabban — children under the age of bar mitzvah

toiva (Yid.) — favor

Torah — the written and oral law given by God to Moses

treif — nonkosher

tzaddi — letter of the Hebrew alphabet

tzaddik — righteous man

tzedakah — charity

tzelem Elokim — the image of God

V

vasikin minyan — early morning prayer service

Vav Adar — sixth of Adar

ve'ahavta lerei'acha kamocha — love your fellow as yourself

Y

yarmulke (Yid.) — skullcap; head covering worn by religious Jewish men

Yerushalayim — Jerusalem

yetzer hara — evil inclination

yetzias Mitzrayim — the Exodus from Egypt

Yiddishkeit (Yid.) — Judaism

yingele (Yid.) — boy

yiras Shamayim — fear of Heaven

yishuv — settlement

Yom Kippur — the Day of Atonement

yom tov — Jewish holiday

Z

zechus (pl. *zechuyos*) — merit

zemiros — Sabbath songs

zichronam livrachah — of blessed memory

About the Author

Rivkah Leah Jacobs resides in Jerusalem with her family. She is a proud mother and grandmother. By profession she is a fine arts teacher, but since making aliyah in 1979, she has mainly taught English and some art history. Together with her husband, Yeshaya, she runs the Artzeinu Tours Travel Agency, providing hotels and tours for religious clientele.

When she was in high school she loved to write, especially poetry; however, she never submitted her work for publication. Approximately four years ago, she committed herself to writing a book to inspire others on the subject of *hashgachah peratis*. All of her stories are true. She hopes her readers will find inspiration and then look for the miracles and Divine providence in their own lives.